The Mind of Dennis Ritchie

The Untold C Language Journey – Unauthorized

Ahmed Barros

ISBN: 9781779699244
Imprint: Popcorn Sandwich
Copyright © 2024 Ahmed Barros.
All Rights Reserved.

Contents

Introduction

The birth of a genius

Early life and influences

Dennis Ritchie, the brilliant mind behind the creation of the C programming language, was born on September 9, 1941, in Bronxville, New York. From an early age, Ritchie showed an aptitude for mathematics and problem-solving. His parents, Alistair Ritchie and Jean McGee Ritchie, recognized his exceptional talent and encouraged his curiosity and love for learning.

Growing up in a household that valued intellectual pursuits, Ritchie was exposed to a wide range of influences that would shape his future endeavors. His father, Alistair, was a physicist who worked on the Manhattan Project during World War II. Alistair's work in nuclear physics ignited Ritchie's interest in science and technology, and he often engaged in discussions about the latest scientific breakthroughs with his father.

In addition to his father's influence, Ritchie's mother, Jean, was an English teacher who instilled in him a deep appreciation for language and literature. She would often read to him and encourage him to explore different genres of literature. This exposure to the power of words and storytelling would later play a role in Ritchie's ability to communicate complex concepts in a clear and concise manner.

Ritchie's early education further nurtured his passion for mathematics and science. He attended Bronxville High School, where he excelled in his studies and showed a particular interest in mathematics and physics. His high school mathematics teacher recognized his exceptional talent and encouraged him to pursue a career in mathematics or engineering.

In 1960, Ritchie enrolled at Harvard University, where he initially pursued a degree in physics. However, he soon realized that his true passion lay in the emerging field of computer science. At Harvard, he had the opportunity to work with the university's cutting-edge computer systems and began to explore the world of programming.

It was during his time at Harvard that Ritchie first encountered the pioneering work of Alan Turing and John von Neumann. Their groundbreaking contributions to the field of computer science left a lasting impression on Ritchie and sparked his curiosity about the possibilities of programming languages.

Ritchie's exposure to the works of Turing and von Neumann inspired him to delve deeper into the world of computer programming. He started exploring different programming languages and became fascinated by the idea of creating a language that would be more efficient and versatile than existing options.

Influenced by his studies in mathematics and his exposure to the emerging field of computer science, Ritchie began to develop a keen interest in the fundamental principles of programming. He recognized the importance of simplicity and elegance in designing programming languages and strived to create a language that would be both powerful and easy to use.

Little did he know that his journey was only just beginning. The birth of the C language and his collaboration with Ken Thompson would propel Ritchie to new heights and forever change the landscape of computer science.

But that is a story for the next chapter. For now, let us reflect on the early life and influences that shaped the mind of Dennis Ritchie, setting him on a path to revolutionize the world of programming.

Family background and upbringing

Dennis Ritchie, the brilliant mind behind the creation of the C language, was born into a family of intellectuals and innovators. His family background and upbringing played a crucial role in shaping his passion for technology and programming.

Dennis was born on September 9, 1941, in Bronxville, New York. His father, Alistair E. Ritchie, was a mathematician and a professional engineer, known for his contributions to the field of numerical analysis. Alistair's passion for logic and problem-solving had a profound impact on Dennis from an early age. Dennis inherited his father's analytical thinking and love for mathematics, laying the foundation for his future achievements.

On the other hand, Dennis's mother, Jean McGee Ritchie, had a background in English literature and teaching. Jean inspired Dennis with her creativity and instilled in him a love for literature and language. Her influence would later contribute to his ability to express complex concepts in a concise and elegant manner, a characteristic that would become a hallmark of the C language.

Growing up in an intellectually stimulating environment, Dennis Ritchie was encouraged to explore his interests and pursue knowledge. His parents fostered an atmosphere of curiosity and provided him with abundant resources to satisfy his thirst for learning. Whether it was books on mathematics, science, or programming, Dennis had access to a wide range of educational materials that fueled his intellectual growth.

In his early years, Dennis spent countless hours tinkering with gadgets and electronics. His parents supported his passion by providing him with electronic kits, which he eagerly assembled and programmed. This hands-on experience allowed him to develop a keen understanding of the inner workings of machines, and fostered his love for coding.

Dennis Ritchie attended carefully selected schools that nurtured his intellectual potential. He demonstrated exceptional aptitude in mathematics, often standing out amongst his peers. His remarkable problem-solving ability and logical reasoning set him apart from his classmates, even at a young age.

Outside of his academic pursuits, Dennis had a vibrant social life. He formed enduring friendships with like-minded individuals who shared his interest in science and technology. Together, they explored the possibilities of early computing and exchanged ideas, further fueling Dennis's passion for programming.

The supportive and intellectually stimulating environment provided by his family and social circle played a crucial role in Dennis Ritchie's development as a programmer. From a young age, he was exposed to the wonders of technology and encouraged to explore his interests. This nurturing upbringing laid the foundation for his later achievements and the groundbreaking contributions he would make to the world of computer science.

Unconventional yet Relevant: The Power of Family in Programming

The influence of family on a person's career path is often overlooked, but in the case of Dennis Ritchie, it played a compelling role. The support, encouragement, and intellectual environment provided by his family not only nurtured his interests but also shaped his perspective on programming.

To truly appreciate the power of family in programming, let's explore a real-world example. Consider the Franklin family: a typical modern-day family with two young siblings, Alice and Ben. Alice is passionate about art and design, while Ben has a natural inclination for problem-solving and logic.

In many families, Alice's artistic pursuits would find plenty of support and resources. She would have access to art classes, workshops, and an abundance of art supplies. Her parents would encourage her creativity, attend her art exhibitions, and celebrate her talent.

However, Ben's interest in programming might not receive the same level of attention. Many parents often equate programming with solitary hours spent in front of a computer screen, lacking social interaction and creativity. This misconception can hinder a child's potential and enthusiasm for programming.

To defy this stereotype, the Franklin family decides to take an unconventional approach. They encourage Alice and Ben to collaborate on projects that combine their interests. They explore the world of digital art, where Ben's programming skills bring Alice's artistic vision to life.

Through this collaboration, Ben develops an understanding of the importance of aesthetics and user experience, while Alice gains an appreciation for the logic and problem-solving involved in programming. The family encourages them to attend programming workshops, provides them with resources, and connects them with mentors who are experts in both programming and art.

As they grow older, Alice and Ben continue to work together on projects that combine their unique skill sets. They develop interactive installations and create innovative applications that blend art and technology. Their collaboration not only enhances their individual talents but also gives rise to groundbreaking creations that captivate audiences.

The Franklin family's unconventional yet relevant approach demonstrates the power of family in programming. By supporting their children's diverse interests and encouraging cross-disciplinary collaboration, they create an environment where programming becomes a tool for creative expression.

This example highlights the impact that a supportive family can have on nurturing interest and talent in programming. It reminds us of the importance of recognizing and valuing diverse interests within a family unit. When parents and siblings encourage and collaborate, they open up new avenues for learning, innovation, and personal growth.

In essence, the power of family lies in creating an atmosphere of support and cross-pollination of ideas. By embracing unconventional approaches and valuing diverse interests, families can unleash the true potential of their budding programmers.

Education and Academic Achievements

Dennis Ritchie's journey towards becoming a programming legend began with his education and academic achievements. From a young age, he displayed an insatiable curiosity and passion for learning, which laid the foundation for his future success in the world of computer science.

1.1.3.1 Early Education: Curiosity Ignited

Growing up in Bronxville, New York, Dennis Ritchie attended local schools where he quickly stood out as an extraordinarily intelligent and inquisitive student. His love for mathematics and science was evident from a young age, and his teachers recognized his exceptional talent and encouraged his thirst for knowledge.

Ritchie's early education provided him with a solid background in mathematics and problem-solving, fostering a logical and analytical mindset that would serve him well in his later pursuits. He excelled in his academic studies, consistently earning top marks and impressing both his classmates and teachers with his natural abilities.

1.1.3.2 College Years: A Quest for Knowledge

After completing his high school education, Ritchie enrolled at Harvard University in 1960, eager to embark on a new chapter of his academic journey. At Harvard, he pursued a degree in applied mathematics, immersing himself in a rich educational environment and actively participating in various mathematics and computer science courses.

During his time at Harvard, Ritchie's passion for programming was ignited. He was captivated by the emerging field of computer science and the endless possibilities it presented. His innate talent for problem-solving and his love for mathematics made him a natural fit for the world of programming.

1.1.3.3 Graduate Studies: Shaping the Future

Following the completion of his undergraduate studies, Ritchie's thirst for knowledge led him to pursue a PhD in mathematics at Harvard University. It was during this period that he began exploring the world of computer programming in greater depth.

Ritchie's graduate studies allowed him to delve into the intricate details of programming languages and algorithms. His research focused on developing efficient algorithms for numerical analysis, showcasing his ability to combine mathematical theory with practical problem-solving skills.

1.1.3.4 Bell Labs: The Crossroads of Innovation

After leaving Harvard without completing his PhD, Ritchie joined the famed Bell Labs in 1967, marking a turning point in his career. At Bell Labs, he found an environment that fostered groundbreaking research and provided him with the resources and support needed to transform his innovative ideas into reality.

While at Bell Labs, Ritchie continued to pursue his passion for programming and contribute to the emerging field of computer science. His collaboration with Ken Thompson resulted in the development of the Unix operating system and the creation of the C programming language, forever changing the course of computing history.

1.1.3.5 Academic Achievements: Leaving a Lasting Legacy

Throughout his illustrious career, Ritchie made significant academic contributions that solidified his reputation as a pioneering figure in computer science. His work on the development of the C programming language, alongside his contributions to the Unix operating system, earned him widespread recognition.

Ritchie's groundbreaking research and innovations not only revolutionized programming languages but also propelled computer science into a new era of versatility and efficiency. His academic achievements continue to shape the way programmers approach software development, inspiring generations of aspiring computer scientists to push the boundaries of what is possible.

In summary, Dennis Ritchie's education and academic achievements played a crucial role in shaping him into the brilliant programmer he became. Starting from his early education, his natural curiosity and exceptional talent were nurtured, leading him to pursue a degree in applied mathematics at Harvard. His experience at Bell Labs and subsequent contributions to the field solidified his reputation as a trailblazer in computer science. Ritchie's academic journey serves as an inspiration to aspiring programmers, highlighting the importance of intellectual curiosity and a thirst for knowledge in making significant contributions to the world of technology.

First encounters with computers

Dennis Ritchie's first encounters with computers were instrumental in shaping his path towards becoming one of the most influential programmers in history. As a young boy, he became fascinated with mathematics and problem-solving, which eventually led him to the world of computing.

Ritchie's early exposure to computers came during his time as a student at Harvard University in the late 1960s. At that time, computers were still relatively rare and expensive machines, limited to academic institutions and large corporations. Ritchie had the opportunity to work with the university's mainframe computer, where he gained hands-on experience that would prove invaluable in his future endeavors.

One of Ritchie's first memorable experiences was programming in Fortran, a high-level programming language widely used for scientific and numerical computations. Using punched cards, Ritchie would write his Fortran programs and submit them to be processed by the mainframe. This process required careful attention to detail, as any mistakes in the punched cards would lead to errors in the program.

It was during this time that Ritchie realized the potential of computers as tools for problem-solving. He was captivated by the power and precision of computers, and he saw programming as a way to harness that power and create solutions to complex problems. This realization sparked his passion for programming and set him on a journey to explore the possibilities of computer science.

Ritchie's early experiences also exposed him to the limitations of existing programming languages. While Fortran was effective for numerical calculations, it was not well-suited for other types of programming tasks. This realization motivated Ritchie to pursue the development of a new programming language that would be more versatile and efficient.

These early encounters with computers provided Ritchie with invaluable insights into the world of programming and set the stage for his future contributions to the field. His experiences with Fortran and the limitations of existing programming languages fueled his desire to create something better – a language that would revolutionize the way software was developed and written.

Little did Ritchie know that these early encounters would become the foundation for his groundbreaking work in the development of the C language and the Unix operating system. His journey was just beginning, and the world of programming was about to be forever changed.

Developing a passion for programming

Dennis Ritchie's journey into the world of programming began at a young age, but it was his innate curiosity and determination that truly set him apart. From tinkering with machines to exploring the depths of computer science, Ritchie's passion for programming was evident from the start.

1. **Early exposure to technology:** Growing up in a technologically inclined household, Ritchie was exposed to computers at an early age. His father, Alistair Ritchie, worked as a physicist and had a deep appreciation for technology. He would often bring home gadgets and electronic devices for Ritchie to experiment with. This early exposure sparked Ritchie's curiosity and laid the foundation for his future passion.

2. **Curiosity drives exploration:** Ritchie's inquisitive mind led him to explore the inner workings of machines, taking them apart and putting them back together with eagerness. He would spend hours tinkering with his toys, trying to understand the underlying mechanisms that made them function. This natural curiosity laid the groundwork for Ritchie's later achievements in programming.

3. **The allure of problem-solving:** As Ritchie grew older, he found himself drawn to problem-solving. Whether it was puzzling over mechanical issues or tackling complex mathematical problems, he thrived on the challenge of finding solutions. This innate problem-solving ability would later serve him well in the world of programming.

4. **Academic pursuits:** Ritchie's passion for problem-solving led him to pursue academic studies in mathematics and physics. He saw these disciplines as a way to further explore and understand the fundamental principles that govern the world. However, it was during his studies that Ritchie encountered his first true exposure to computers.

5. **The breakthrough:** At Harvard University, Ritchie had the opportunity to work on the university's IBM 704 mainframe computer. This experience was a turning point for him, as it allowed him to delve deeper into the realm of programming. He quickly realized that programming was a way to unleash his creativity and make a tangible impact on the world.

6. **Programming becomes the primary focus:** After his initial exposure to programming, Ritchie's interest in mathematics and physics took a backseat. He was captivated by the world of coding and spent countless hours honing his programming skills. Ritchie's determination to master this new craft became unwavering, and he sought out every opportunity to learn and grow in the field.

7. **Fascination with computer architecture:** One aspect of programming that particularly fascinated Ritchie was computer architecture. He was intrigued by the intricate design of computers and the way they operated on a fundamental level. This fascination motivated him to dive deeper into the inner workings of machines and become an expert in computer systems.

8. **The joy of computational thinking:** As Ritchie delved further into programming, he discovered the joy of computational thinking. He realized that programming was not just about writing code, but about approaching problems analytically and devising efficient and elegant solutions. This shift in mindset only fueled his passion and commitment to the field.

9. **Collaborative spirit:** Ritchie's love for programming was not limited to his personal pursuits. He found immense joy and satisfaction in collaborating with others to solve complex problems. Whether it was working with classmates on programming assignments or collaborating with colleagues on groundbreaking projects, Ritchie thrived in a team environment where ideas could be shared and explored.

10. **The birth of a lifelong passion:** As Ritchie's knowledge and expertise in programming grew, so did his passion for the field. Programming became more than just a career path for him; it became a lifelong passion. Ritchie would go on to

revolutionize programming languages and make significant contributions to the world of computer science, all fueled by his unwavering love for programming.

In conclusion, Dennis Ritchie's journey into programming was marked by a natural curiosity, problem-solving abilities, and a relentless passion for exploring the world of computers. From his early exposure to technology to his transformative experiences at Harvard University, Ritchie's path was paved with curiosity, determination, and a deep love for the art of programming. It is this passion that would propel him to become one of the most influential programmers of our time, leaving an indelible mark on computer science.

The dawn of a new era

The birth of the C language

In the vast landscape of computer programming, there are few languages that can truly claim to have shaped the foundation of modern computing. One such language is C, which has left an indelible mark on the world of software development. The story of C's birth is an intriguing one, filled with collaboration, innovation, and a deep desire to create a language that would revolutionize programming.

To understand the birth of the C language, we must delve into the early days of computer science and the emergence of high-level programming languages. In the 1960s, languages like Fortran and COBOL were popular, but they were limited in their capabilities and lacked the flexibility required for certain types of programming tasks. This limitation sparked a desire for a new language that would bridge the gap between low-level machine code and high-level languages.

1.2.1 Early struggles and the need for a new language Dennis Ritchie, a brilliant computer scientist working at Bell Labs, recognized these limitations and became determined to create a language that could overcome them. His initial attempts led to a language called B, which was a precursor to C. However, B had its own set of limitations and was not powerful enough to fulfill Ritchie's vision.

Ritchie, along with his colleague Ken Thompson, realized that they needed to build a new language from scratch to address these shortcomings. They wanted a language that would be simple, efficient, and versatile enough to handle a wide range of programming tasks. And so, the journey to create the C language began.

1.2.2 The collaboration of Dennis Ritchie and Ken Thompson Ritchie's collaboration with Ken Thompson proved to be instrumental in the development of the C language. They brought together their combined expertise, with Ritchie focusing on the language design and Thomson working on the implementation.

The duo worked tirelessly, spending countless hours discussing, coding, and refining their ideas. They wanted to create a language that would provide low-level control like assembly language while also being portable and easy to use. This combination of power and simplicity became a guiding principle in the development of C.

1.2.3 Influences from Basic Combined Programming Language (BCPL) Inspiration for C also came from another programming language called BCPL, developed by Martin Richards at the University of Cambridge. BCPL shared several features with C, including its simplicity and ability to generate efficient machine code.

Ritchie and Thompson studied BCPL and saw an opportunity to build upon its strengths while addressing its shortcomings. They borrowed ideas from BCPL, such as the concept of pointers and the use of a concise syntax, and integrated them into the design of C. This borrowing of ideas was not uncommon in the early days of computer science, as collaboration and knowledge sharing were essential for progress.

1.2.4 The birth of the C language After years of refinement and hard work, Ritchie and Thompson finally unveiled the C language in the early 1970s. It was an instant success, capturing the imagination of programmers around the world. With its simplicity, power, and portability, C quickly gained popularity and became the language of choice for system programming, operating systems, and embedded systems.

The name "C" was chosen simply because it succeeded the B language. However, the letter 'C' also conveys a sense of progression and evolution, which perfectly encapsulated the spirit of the language.

1.2.5 The impact of the C language on computer science The birth of the C language marked a significant turning point in the world of computer science. C introduced concepts like structured programming, modularity, and portability, which changed the way programmers approached software development. It provided a level of abstraction that made programming more accessible and removed some of the complexities associated with low-level languages.

Moreover, C served as a foundation for many other programming languages that followed. Languages like C++, Objective-C, and C# were all born out of the C language, each with its own unique features and applications.

Today, C remains one of the most widely used programming languages, powering everything from operating systems to embedded systems to microcontrollers. Its influence and impact continue to reverberate throughout the field of computer science, cementing Ritchie's legacy as one of the greatest minds in programming.

However, the birth of the C language was just the beginning of Ritchie's journey. In the following sections, we will explore the innovations and contributions that he made, as well as the challenges he faced along the way. Through it all, Ritchie's unwavering passion for programming and his commitment to collaboration would continue to shape the course of computer science.

Collaborating with Ken Thompson

In the early 1970s, the world of computing was eager for innovation. It was during this time that Dennis Ritchie embarked on a collaborative journey with his fellow programmer, Ken Thompson, which would ultimately change the landscape of programming forever. Their partnership, characterized by their deep mutual respect and shared passion for computing, gave birth to one of the most influential programming languages in history: C.

Ken Thompson, a brilliant programmer in his own right, had already made a name for himself with his pioneering work on the development of the UNIX operating system. When Thompson and Ritchie crossed paths at the Bell Labs research facility in the late 1960s, it was a meeting of minds that would prove to be truly extraordinary.

Thompson had been developing UNIX, but he recognized the need for a high-level programming language that would allow for efficient system programming. He turned to Ritchie, knowing that his expertise and creativity would be invaluable in tackling this challenge. And so, their collaboration began.

Together, Ritchie and Thompson embarked on a mission to create a language that combined the power and efficiency of low-level assembly languages with the ease of use and portability of high-level languages. Their vision was to create a language that would be both practical and elegant, enabling programmers to write efficient and concise code.

The result of their collaboration was the birth of the C language. Drawing inspiration from earlier languages such as ALGOL, BCPL, and B, Ritchie and Thompson crafted a language that was simple yet powerful, with a focus on efficiency and flexibility. They designed C to give programmers direct access to the underlying hardware while providing high-level features like structured programming, data abstraction, and modularity.

Throughout their collaboration, Ritchie and Thompson faced numerous challenges. They had to strike a delicate balance between simplicity and expressiveness, ensuring that C would be easy to learn and use, while still providing the necessary tools for complex software development. They spent countless hours discussing and refining the syntax, semantics, and features of the language, constantly iterating and improving upon their ideas.

One of the key breakthroughs of their collaboration was the development of the C compiler. This innovative tool translated C code into machine-readable instructions, making it possible to write programs in a high-level language and execute them efficiently on different hardware platforms. The C compiler revolutionized the way software was developed, making it easier to write portable and efficient code.

Another significant contribution of Ritchie and Thompson's collaboration was the concept of machine-independent programming. By designing C to be platform-agnostic, they were able to decouple software development from specific hardware architectures. This allowed programmers to write code that could be compiled and run on different systems, making software more versatile and accessible.

Their groundbreaking work on the C language opened up new horizons in the world of software development. C quickly gained popularity among programmers, becoming the language of choice for system programming, embedded systems, and operating system development. Its simplicity, efficiency, and portability made it a favorite among developers, and its influence began to spread far and wide.

The collaboration between Ritchie and Thompson extended beyond the development of the C language. They also worked together on the creation of the UNIX operating system, which played a significant role in the growth of the open-source movement. UNIX, with its modular design and emphasis on simplicity, became the cornerstone of modern operating systems and laid the foundation for the development of Linux and other open-source projects.

Throughout their collaboration, Ritchie and Thompson not only shared ideas and expertise but also built a culture of collaboration at Bell Labs. They fostered an environment where programmers were encouraged to exchange knowledge and work together to solve complex problems. Their collaborative approach proved to be instrumental in driving innovation and pushing the boundaries of what was possible in software development.

In conclusion, the collaboration between Dennis Ritchie and Ken Thompson was a defining moment in the history of programming. Their partnership gave birth to the C language, revolutionizing the way software was developed and opening up new possibilities for programmers. Through their shared vision and commitment to excellence, Ritchie and Thompson left an indelible mark on the world of computing and continue to inspire future generations of programmers.

University of Texas and the development of Unix

The University of Texas played a significant role in the development of Unix, a groundbreaking operating system that revolutionized the field of computer science. In this section, we will explore the pivotal contributions made by Dennis Ritchie during his time at the university and the subsequent development of Unix.

The Birth of Unix at Bell Labs

Before delving into Ritchie's time at the University of Texas, it is essential to understand the origins of Unix. Unix was initially developed at Bell Labs in the early 1970s by Ritchie and his colleague Ken Thompson. It was a response to the limitations of the operating systems of that era, which were tied to specific hardware architectures.

Unix introduced a novel approach to operating systems by utilizing a modular design and a simple yet powerful command-line interface. It prioritized flexibility, portability, and the concept of "everything is a file." This design philosophy allowed Unix to run on a wide range of hardware platforms, making it highly adaptable and widely accessible.

Ritchie's Transition to the University of Texas

In 1967, Ritchie completed his Ph.D. in mathematics at Harvard University and joined Bell Labs, where he began working on the Multics project. Multics aimed to develop a time-sharing operating system that could support multiple users simultaneously. Although Multics was not entirely successful, it provided the foundation for the development of Unix.

In the early 1970s, Ritchie took a sabbatical from Bell Labs and joined the Computing Science Research Center at the University of Texas. This transition proved to be pivotal in the development of Unix as Ritchie had the opportunity to further refine and expand upon his ideas. At the University of Texas, he collaborated with colleagues and students who shared his passion for computing, including Doug McIlroy and Rudd Canaday.

Innovation and Collaboration at the University of Texas

Ritchie and his collaborators at the University of Texas made substantial contributions to the development of Unix. They focused on improving the system's scalability, performance, and user interface. One of the most important advancements during this period was the implementation of the pipes and filters mechanism, which allowed for seamless inter-process communication.

Additionally, Ritchie and his colleagues introduced a number of fundamental Unix utilities, such as the "grep" command for pattern matching and the "ls" command for directory listing. These utilities exemplified the Unix philosophy of creating small, specialized tools that could be combined to solve complex problems, a concept that still persists in modern software development.

Impact on the University and Beyond

Ritchie's time at the University of Texas had a lasting impact not only on the development of Unix but also on the academic community. The university became a hub for Unix research and development, attracting talented individuals who went on to make significant contributions to the field.

The collaborative and open nature of Unix development at the University of Texas laid the foundation for the open-source movement that followed. The ethos of sharing and collaboration cultivated during this time continues to influence the software industry today.

The Enduring Legacy

The contributions made by Dennis Ritchie and his colleagues at the University of Texas shaped the future of operating systems and programming. Unix became a foundational system and provided the inspiration for subsequent operating systems such as Linux and macOS. The principles of simplicity, modularity, and portability that Ritchie championed continue to guide the design of modern software systems.

It is crucial to acknowledge the profound impact that the University of Texas had on the development of Unix. The atmosphere of innovation and collaboration fostered at the university laid the groundwork for the transformative advancements in computing that followed. The legacy of Ritchie's work and the Unix operating system serve as a testament to the enduring power of visionary ideas and the importance of collaboration in pushing the boundaries of what is possible in the world of technology.

Challenges and the Spirit of Innovation

Throughout his career, Ritchie faced numerous challenges, both technical and cultural. The development of Unix itself was not without obstacles. Limited computational resources necessitated creativity and resourcefulness in implementing various features. Moreover, Unix initially faced skepticism and resistance from established computing institutions.

However, Ritchie's innovative mindset and relentless pursuit of excellence helped overcome these challenges. His ability to balance theoretical knowledge with practical considerations allowed him to create a system that was both elegant and efficient. The impact of Unix on the field of computer science is a testament to Ritchie's vision and perseverance.

Real-World Problem: Portability and Interoperability

One of the key challenges addressed by Ritchie and his collaborators was the issue of portability and interoperability in operating systems. Prior to Unix, operating systems were typically tied to specific hardware platforms, making it difficult to develop software that could run on multiple systems.

Unix's design philosophy of abstraction and machine independence allowed it to be ported to different hardware architectures. This meant that software written for one Unix system could be easily executed on another without significant modifications. This portability was crucial in fostering collaboration and enabling the widespread adoption of Unix.

Today, portability and interoperability remain essential considerations in software development. Developers often need to ensure that their applications can run seamlessly across different operating systems and hardware platforms. By understanding the principles underlying Unix's portability, modern programmers can design software that is both platform-independent and compatible with a wide range of systems.

Further Exploration: The Unix Philosophy

Another fascinating aspect of Unix, which shaped its development at the University of Texas, is the Unix philosophy. The Unix philosophy emphasizes simplicity, modularity, and the composition of smaller tools to accomplish complex tasks.

As a practitioner of the Unix philosophy, Ritchie believed in creating software that performed a single task well and was highly composable. This approach encouraged reusability and modularity, laying the groundwork for modern software engineering practices such as microservices and component-based development.

Exploring the Unix philosophy in more depth can provide valuable insights into designing modular and maintainable software systems. By decomposing complex systems into smaller, independently testable components, developers can create more robust and scalable software architectures.

Summary

In summary, during his time at the University of Texas, Dennis Ritchie made significant contributions to the development of Unix, refining its design, and contributing several groundbreaking utilities. The collaborative environment at the university played a vital role in fostering innovation and solidifying Unix's place as a transformative operating system.

Ritchie's work at the University of Texas demonstrated the power of collaboration, the importance of portability and interoperability, and the enduring influence of the Unix philosophy. The development of Unix at the University of Texas serves as a testament to the impact that a dedicated group of individuals can have on the world of computer science.

The evolution of the C language

The birth of the C language marked the beginning of a new era in programming. Developed by Dennis Ritchie and originally designed to improve upon the limitations of assembly language, C quickly evolved into a powerful and versatile programming language. In this section, we will explore the various stages of the C language's evolution, from its early versions to the current standards.

1. The birth of C: Initially developed in the early 1970s, C originated as an extension of the B programming language, which was itself a modification of the BCPL language. The goal was to create a language that offered high-level abstractions while still providing low-level control over the hardware. This balance became the defining characteristic of C and the key to its widespread adoption.

2. K&R C: The first formal definition of the C language was presented in the book "The C Programming Language" by Brian Kernighan and Dennis Ritchie, commonly referred to as K&R C. This book, published in 1978, not only served as a manual for learning C but also solidified the language's syntax and semantics. K&R C laid the foundation for future versions and became the standard reference for C programmers.

3. ANSI C: In the early 1980s, the American National Standards Institute (ANSI) undertook the task of standardizing the C language. The result was the ANSI C standard, published in 1989. This standard introduced significant improvements and refinements to the language, providing a more robust and

unified specification. It also introduced standard library functions, such as those defined in "stdio.h" and "stdlib.h", which became essential for C programming.

4. ISO C: The International Organization for Standardization (ISO) also recognized the importance of standardizing C and adopted the ANSI C standard as ISO/IEC 9899:1990. This standard, commonly known as ISO C or C89, further solidified the language's specifications and extended its reach to a global audience. ISO C brought greater portability and compatibility to C programs across different platforms.

5. C99: In 1999, ISO/IEC published the C99 standard, which introduced several significant additions to the language. This version introduced new data types, enhanced support for complex numbers and variable-length arrays, improved support for inline functions, and introduced new standard library functions. Additionally, C99 relaxed some of the constraints on variable declarations, making code more concise and readable.

6. C11: The most recent version of the C language standard, published in 2011, is known as C11. This revision introduced several new features and improvements to the language. Notable additions include support for multithreading, improved Unicode support, new library functions for safer string manipulation, and improved support for atomic operations. C11 further solidified C's status as a modern and relevant programming language.

While the evolution of the C language has brought about significant improvements and increased its functionality, it is important to note that the core principles of the language have remained intact. C still prioritizes efficiency, control, and simplicity, making it an ideal choice for system programming, embedded systems, and applications that require direct hardware access.

Despite the introduction of newer programming languages, C continues to be widely used and forms the basis for many other high-level programming languages, such as C++, Objective-C, and Java. The resilience and adaptability of the C language speak to its enduring relevance and the legacy of Dennis Ritchie's visionary work.

C Language Pioneers One of the strengths of the C language is the vibrant programming community that has grown around it. Many renowned programmers have made significant contributions to the language's evolution. Here are some of the prominent figures in the development of the C language:

1. Dennis Ritchie: As the co-creator of the C language, Dennis Ritchie played a pivotal role in the language's invention and its subsequent evolution. His work on the C compiler and the development of Unix cemented his status as one of the most influential programmers of his time.

2. Brian Kernighan: Alongside Ritchie, Kernighan co-authored "The C Programming Language" and contributed immensely to the early development of C. He also coined the term "Hello, World!" in the book, which has since become the standard first program for beginners learning a new programming language.

3. Bjarne Stroustrup: Building upon the foundation of C, Bjarne Stroustrup created C++, a powerful extension of the C language. C++ introduced object-oriented programming capabilities and expanded the possibilities for software development.

4. James Gosling: Gosling is best known for his work on the Java programming language. Java borrows syntax from C and C++ while adding new features and a platform-independent execution model. Gosling's contributions to the C language helped shape the design of Java.

5. Linus Torvalds: While not directly involved in the creation of the C language, Torvalds made significant contributions to the development of the Linux operating system. Linux relies heavily on the C language, and Torvalds' work has further advanced the possibilities of C in the context of operating systems.

The evolution of the C language has been driven by the collaborative efforts of these visionary programmers and the wider programming community. Their contributions have transformed C into a powerful and versatile programming language that continues to shape the field of computer science.

The impact of the C language on computer science

The birth of the C language marked a turning point in the history of computer science. Its impact on the field cannot be overstated, as it revolutionized programming languages and laid the foundation for the development of modern software systems.

1. The development of the C compiler:

The development of the C language was accompanied by the creation of the first C compiler by Dennis Ritchie himself. This compiler allowed programmers to write C code and translate it into machine-readable instructions, making programming more accessible and efficient. The C compiler's ability to generate highly optimized code helped improve the performance of software applications.

2. The concept of machine-independent programming:

One of the most significant contributions of the C language was the concept of machine-independent programming. Before C, programmers had to write code specifically for each computer system. However, C introduced portability and allowed programs to be written once and run on different platforms with minimal modifications. This breakthrough significantly simplified software development and reduced the cost and time required to bring software to market.

3. The significance of the C language in the software industry:

The C language quickly gained popularity in the software industry due to its simplicity, efficiency, and versatility. Its syntax was easy to learn and understand, making it accessible to both novice and experienced programmers. Its efficiency in terms of both execution speed and memory usage made it ideal for developing system software such as operating systems, compilers, and device drivers.

4. The influence of C on other programming languages:

The impact of the C language extends beyond its own success. Many modern programming languages, including C++, Java, and Python, have been influenced by the design principles and syntax of C. C++, in particular, was developed as an extension of C to provide additional features such as object-oriented programming. The widespread adoption of these languages can be attributed, in part, to the foundation laid by the C language.

5. Ritchie's contributions to standardization efforts:

Dennis Ritchie played a crucial role in standardizing the C language. He worked with the American National Standards Institute (ANSI) to develop a standardized version of C, known as ANSI C or C89. This standardization ensured that C programs written in one environment would run correctly on other compliant platforms. The introduction of standards helped further establish C as a reliable and widely accepted programming language.

The impact of the C language on computer science is undeniable. Its simplicity, efficiency, and portability have shaped the way programmers approach software development. The C language serves as a bridge between hardware and software, allowing programmers to harness the power of computer systems and build robust and reliable applications.

However, it is important to note that the C language is not without its challenges. Its flexibility and low-level nature require programmers to exercise caution and adhere to good programming practices to avoid security vulnerabilities and memory-related issues. Nonetheless, the impact of the C language on computer science remains a testament to Dennis Ritchie's genius and his ability to create a language that continues to influence generations of programmers.

Interactions with other sections

This section on the impact of the C language on computer science is closely tied to the earlier section on the birth of the C language (Section 1.2.1). While the birth of the C language focuses on the historical context and the collaboration between Dennis

Ritchie and Ken Thompson, the impact section delves deeper into the lasting effects of their creation.

Additionally, this section connects to the section on the revolutionizing of programming languages (Section 2.1). The discussion of the C language's influence on other programming languages demonstrates its role in shaping the larger programming landscape.

Furthermore, the impact of the C language on computer science is relevant to the section on the role of C in the development of operating systems (Section 4.1.2). By highlighting the portability and efficiency of C, we can explore how it served as a foundational language for developing operating systems like Unix.

Finally, this section contributes to the overall theme of the book by emphasizing the enduring legacy of Dennis Ritchie (Section 5.1). By showcasing the impact of the C language, we reinforce Ritchie's importance and influence in the field of computer science and programming.

Chapter Two: Innovations and Contributions

Revolutionizing programming languages

The concept of machine-independent programming

The concept of machine-independent programming is at the core of the C language's revolutionary impact on computer science and software development. This concept refers to the ability to write code that can be executed on different computer systems without any modifications or adaptations.

In the early days of computing, each computer system had its own unique assembly language specific to its hardware architecture. This meant that programmers had to write separate versions of their code for each different computer system they wanted their program to run on. This was not only time-consuming and tedious but also limited the portability and scalability of software.

Dennis Ritchie saw this limitation as an opportunity and set out to create a programming language that would allow developers to write code once and have it run on multiple systems without modification. His vision was to enable the development of software that could be easily ported from one computer system to another, regardless of the underlying hardware.

To achieve machine independence, Ritchie designed the C language with a set of fundamental principles and features. One of the key principles was to create a language that is close to the hardware, providing low-level control while also being portable. This resulted in a language that strikes a balance between high-level abstraction and low-level control, making it suitable for system-level programming as well as application development.

The C language achieves machine independence through several key features:

Abstraction from hardware-specific details

C abstracts the low-level hardware details, such as memory organization and CPU registers, through its syntax and standard library. This allows programmers to write code that is portable across different hardware architectures, as long as the underlying systems support the C language.

Standardized data types and sizes

C provides a set of standardized data types with fixed sizes, such as int, float, double, etc. This ensures that the same code will produce consistent results on different systems, regardless of the underlying hardware or operating system. For example, an int variable will always have a size of 4 bytes, regardless of whether it is running on a 32-bit or 64-bit system.

Transparent memory management

C puts the responsibility of memory management on the programmer, providing features such as pointers and manual memory allocation through functions like malloc and free. This allows programmers to have fine-grained control over the memory usage and allocation, making it possible to write efficient code that can adapt to different hardware configurations.

Control over system resources

C provides direct access to system resources, such as files, input/output operations, and hardware peripherals. This allows programmers to write code that can interact with the underlying system without being tied to a specific hardware configuration. For example, a C program can read and write files regardless of the file system used by the operating system.

Standardized function libraries

C includes a rich set of standard libraries, such as the C Standard Library, that provide a wide range of functions for common tasks. These libraries abstract the underlying system-specific implementations, making it easier to develop portable code that can run on different systems without modification.

The concept of machine-independent programming revolutionized the software industry by enabling the development of portable, scalable, and efficient software. It allowed programmers to write code that could be easily ported to different systems, reducing development time and increasing cross-platform compatibility.

With the advent of the C language and its machine-independent programming capabilities, software developers no longer had to restrict themselves to a specific hardware platform. They could write code that could run on a wide range of systems, from microcontrollers to mainframes, without the need for extensive modifications.

This concept continues to be relevant today, as the C language remains a popular choice for system-level programming, embedded systems, and operating system development. The principles of machine-independent programming, as exemplified by the C language, have also influenced the design and development of other programming languages, ensuring that the concept continues to shape the future of computer science.

Example: Let's consider a scenario where a software company wants to develop a graphics rendering library. In the past, they would have to write separate versions of the library for different hardware platforms, such as Windows, macOS, and Linux. Each version would require a significant amount of time and effort to adapt the code to the specific system architecture.

However, with the advent of machine-independent programming and the availability of the C language, the company can now write a single codebase for their graphics rendering library. This codebase can then be compiled and executed on different systems without modification, as long as the systems support the C language.

By adopting machine-independent programming principles, the company can significantly reduce development time and costs. They can also ensure that their library is accessible to a wider audience, as it can be used on different systems without requiring separate versions.

In summary, the concept of machine-independent programming, as realized in the C language, has transformed the software industry by allowing code to be written once and executed on different systems. This concept continues to shape the development of software and serves as a reminder of Dennis Ritchie's vision for a more portable and scalable future in programming.

The significance of the C language in the software industry

The C language has had a profound impact on the software industry since its inception. Its simplicity, power, and versatility have made it a favorite among programmers, and its widespread adoption has shaped the development of computer systems and software applications.

One of the key reasons for the significance of the C language in the software industry is its ability to offer low-level and high-level programming constructs. C allows programmers to write code that directly interacts with the hardware, making it a suitable language for system programming, embedded systems, and device drivers. At the same time, it provides high-level abstractions, such as functions and data structures, which make it a versatile language for developing software applications.

The efficiency of the C language is another factor that has contributed to its significance. C code can be compiled and executed with minimal overhead, making it an ideal choice for performance-critical applications. Its minimalistic approach to programming enables tight control over system resources and efficient memory management, allowing programmers to optimize their code for speed and size.

The portability of the C language is another attribute that has made it indispensable in the software industry. C code can be easily adapted to run on different platforms without significant modifications, thanks to the presence of numerous compilers and libraries that support the language. This portability has allowed software developers to create cross-platform applications and system software, making C a lingua franca of sorts in the industry.

Moreover, the C language has served as a foundation for the development of numerous other programming languages. Many modern languages, such as C++, Java, and Python, have borrowed syntax and concepts from C, making it easier for programmers to transition between different languages. The influence of C can be seen in the design of these languages, particularly in their support for structured programming and object-oriented programming paradigms.

The C language's impact on the software industry extends beyond its technical capabilities. It has played a significant role in fostering a community of programmers who adhere to certain coding standards and practices. Its emphasis on simplicity, efficiency, and modularity has influenced the way software is developed and maintained. The widespread use of C in open-source projects has further fostered collaboration and knowledge sharing among software developers.

In order to understand the significance of the C language in the software industry, it is essential to recognize its role in shaping the evolution of computer systems. The C language was instrumental in the development of Unix, an operating system that revolutionized the field of computing. Unix, written in C, provided an elegant and powerful environment for software development and became the basis for many modern operating systems, including Linux.

The impact of the C language can also be seen in various domains of software development. From embedded systems and game programming to scientific computation and web development, the C language has found applications in a wide range of fields. Its versatility and performance have enabled the creation of complex and robust software solutions that power industries and businesses worldwide.

To illustrate the significance of the C language in the software industry, let us consider a real-world example. Imagine a team of programmers developing a new operating system for a mobile device. By using the C language, they can write efficient and portable code that interacts directly with the device's hardware. They can leverage the simplicity and power of C to implement low-level functionalities, such as memory management and process scheduling, while also utilizing high-level abstractions to build user-friendly applications on top of the operating system. The portability of C allows their code to be easily adapted to different mobile platforms, and its efficiency ensures that the operating system runs smoothly on resource-constrained devices.

In conclusion, the significance of the C language in the software industry cannot be overstated. Its simplicity, power, efficiency, portability, and versatility have made it a staple language for software development. The impact of C extends beyond technical considerations and has shaped the way software is developed, maintained, and shared. Its influence can be seen in the design of modern programming languages and the development of computer systems. As the software industry continues to evolve, the lessons and principles of the C language remain relevant, making it a timeless and indispensable tool for programmers.

The influence of C on other programming languages

The development of the C language by Dennis Ritchie has had a profound impact on the world of programming, influencing numerous other programming languages and shaping the way software is developed. In this section, we will explore the key ways in which C has influenced other programming languages and discuss the lasting legacy of its design principles.

The simplicity and elegance of C

One of the most significant aspects of C that has influenced other programming languages is its simplicity and elegance. C was designed to be a low-level language that allows for efficient and concise programming, making it accessible to both experienced and novice programmers. This emphasis on simplicity has been carried forward into many modern programming languages, including C++, Java, and Python.

The syntax of C, with its minimalistic and straightforward structure, has become a blueprint for many subsequent programming languages. Features such as the use of curly braces for code blocks, semicolons to terminate statements, and the ability to define variables and functions have become ubiquitous in the programming world.

C's influence can also be seen in the adoption of similar control flow constructs, such as loops and conditional statements, in languages like Java and C#.

Portability and platform independence

C introduced the concept of machine-independent programming, allowing developers to write code that could be easily ported across different hardware architectures and operating systems. This concept of platform independence has become a central tenet of many popular programming languages.

For example, C++ was designed as an extension of C to provide object-oriented programming while maintaining the portability of C. Java, another language heavily influenced by C, took this idea even further by implementing the principle of "write once, run anywhere." Java code is compiled into bytecode, which can be executed on any platform that has a Java Virtual Machine (JVM). This approach has enabled Java to become one of the most widely used programming languages for web and enterprise applications.

Performance and efficiency

C was designed to be a language that strikes a balance between high-level language convenience and low-level language efficiency. This emphasis on performance has been carried forward into many other programming languages, particularly those used in systems programming and embedded systems.

Languages like C++ and Rust have built upon C's performance-focused design principles while providing higher-level abstractions. C++ introduces features such as classes, templates, and exceptions, which allow developers to write safer and more maintainable code without sacrificing performance. Rust, on the other hand, takes inspiration from C's control over memory management while offering stronger memory safety guarantees.

Influence on object-oriented programming

C's influence on object-oriented programming (OOP) cannot be overstated. While C itself is not an object-oriented language, it provided the foundation for the development of many object-oriented languages that followed.

C++ was developed as an extension of C, adding support for classes, inheritance, and polymorphism. These features revolutionized the world of software development by providing a more modular and reusable approach to programming. Languages such as Java, C#, and Python have also embraced object-oriented programming and have taken inspiration from C++ in their syntax and design.

Legacy and future directions

The influence of C on other programming languages goes beyond just its technical features. C introduced a new way of thinking about software development, emphasizing simplicity, efficiency, and portability. These principles have shaped the software industry and continue to influence the direction of programming languages today.

As technology evolves, new programming languages continue to be developed, building upon the foundations set by C. The influence of C can be seen in languages such as Go, Swift, and Rust, which aim to combine the best aspects of C with modern language features.

In conclusion, the impact of C on other programming languages cannot be understated. Its simplicity, portability, performance, and influence on object-oriented programming have shaped the way software is developed and continue to drive innovation in the field. As programmers, we owe a debt of gratitude to Dennis Ritchie for his pioneering work in creating the C language and setting the stage for the future of programming.

Ritchie's Contributions to Standardization Efforts

In addition to his groundbreaking work on the C language and the development of Unix, Dennis Ritchie made significant contributions to the standardization efforts in the software industry. His efforts focused on establishing a set of guidelines and conventions for programming languages and software development practices. Let us explore some of Ritchie's key contributions to standardization in more detail.

Defining the ANSI C Standard

One of Ritchie's most notable contributions to standardization was his involvement in the development of the ANSI C Standard. ANSI C, also known as the C89 Standard, aimed to establish a common set of rules and features for the C programming language. As a member of the ANSI X3J11 committee, Ritchie played a crucial role in shaping the standard.

The ANSI C Standard helped promote portability and compatibility of C code across different platforms and compilers. It defined the syntax, semantics, and libraries of the C language, providing a uniform framework for C programmers to follow. By establishing a standardized version of C, Ritchie facilitated collaboration and interoperability within the programming community and enabled the growth of C as a widely used language.

Influencing the POSIX Standard

Apart from his contributions to the C language standard, Ritchie also had a significant impact on the POSIX (Portable Operating System Interface) standard. POSIX aimed to define a set of APIs (Application Programming Interfaces) that would enable software to be easily ported across different operating systems.

Ritchie's expertise in operating systems, particularly his work on Unix, made him a valuable contributor to the POSIX standardization process. His insights and technical knowledge helped shape the standard and ensure its compatibility with Unix-like systems.

By contributing to the POSIX standard, Ritchie facilitated the development of cross-platform software and encouraged collaboration between different operating system vendors. The standardization of APIs enabled programmers to write code that could run on multiple operating systems without major modifications, saving time and effort in software development.

Promoting Interoperability and Code Reusability

Ritchie's contributions to standardization efforts went beyond defining language and operating system standards. He also emphasized the importance of interoperability and code reusability in software development.

Ritchie advocated for the development of well-documented, consistent APIs and libraries that would enable programmers to reuse code more easily. His belief in modular programming and the use of standard interfaces helped promote code sharing and collaboration among programmers.

By standardizing APIs and promoting code reusability, Ritchie facilitated the creation of software libraries and frameworks that could be leveraged by multiple projects. This approach not only improved the efficiency of software development but also encouraged the growth of a vibrant ecosystem of software components that could be easily integrated into various applications.

Addressing Challenges and Ensuring Compatibility

Throughout his career, Ritchie addressed numerous challenges in the standardization of programming languages and software development practices. He focused on balancing innovation with practicality, recognizing the importance of backward compatibility and ensuring smooth transitions between different versions and implementations.

Ritchie's approach to standardization involved rigorous testing, documentation, and collaboration with the programming community. He actively sought feedback and input from fellow programmers and industry experts, incorporating their insights into the development of standards.

By addressing challenges and ensuring compatibility, Ritchie's contributions to standardization efforts helped create a stable foundation for software development. His emphasis on compatibility and practicality continues to influence modern standardization efforts, ensuring that software remains accessible, maintainable, and compatible across different platforms and environments.

Real-World Example: The Impact of Standardization

To understand the significance of Ritchie's contributions to standardization, let us consider a real-world example: the development of web browsers. Web browsers need to interpret HTML and CSS code written by web developers and display web pages consistently across different devices and operating systems.

Thanks to the standardization efforts in programming languages like C and the definition of web standards by organizations such as the World Wide Web Consortium (W3C), web browsers can execute code written in a standardized manner. This consistency ensures that websites look and function the same regardless of the browser or device used.

Ritchie's contributions to standardization, by establishing guidelines and conventions, have had a cascading effect on various aspects of software development. They have not only facilitated code reuse and interoperability but also enabled the creation of complex software systems that can integrate seamlessly with other technologies.

Additional Resources

If you are interested in learning more about Ritchie's contributions to standardization efforts and the impact of standardization on software development, the following resources are highly recommended:

1. "The C Programming Language," by Brian W. Kernighan and Dennis M. Ritchie: This book, written by Ritchie himself, provides a comprehensive guide to the C language and its standardization efforts.

2. "The Art of UNIX Programming," by Eric S. Raymond: This book explores the philosophy and culture behind Unix and the impact of standardization on the Unix ecosystem.

3. "Programming Language Pragmatics," by Michael L. Scott: This book offers an in-depth look at the design and implementation of programming languages, including the role of standardization in language development.

4. "The Standard C Library," by P. J. Plauger: This book delves into the standard library for the C programming language, providing insights into the importance of standardization in creating portable code.

These resources will provide you with a deeper understanding of Ritchie's contributions, the principles of standardization, and their impact on the software industry. By leveraging the knowledge gained from these sources, you can further appreciate the value of standardization in software development and carry forward Ritchie's legacy of creating robust and interoperable software systems.

Unix and the rise of the open-source movement

The creation of the Unix operating system

In the early 1960s, Dennis Ritchie found himself intrigued by the challenges and possibilities presented by the emerging field of operating systems. At the time, most computers were large and expensive, making it necessary for multiple users to share the resources of a single machine. However, the existing operating systems were inefficient and lacked the versatility needed to support different types of applications.

Motivated by this problem, Ritchie embarked on a journey to create an operating system that would address these limitations. In collaboration with his colleague Ken Thompson, he set out to develop a system that would be simple, portable, and highly flexible. Little did they know that this ambitious project would revolutionize the world of computing.

The development of the Unix operating system began in 1969 at the Bell Labs research center. Ritchie and Thompson believed that a key aspect of their design should be the use of a high-level programming language, rather than a machine-specific assembly language. They chose to write Unix in the C programming language, which Ritchie had created a few years earlier.

By using C, Ritchie and Thompson were able to develop an operating system that was not tied to any particular hardware architecture. This portability was a crucial factor in Unix's success, as it allowed the system to be easily adapted for different computer systems. It also meant that developers could write software for Unix using a single programming language, rather than having to learn multiple languages for different platforms.

The design principles behind Unix were also groundbreaking. Instead of building a monolithic system, Ritchie and Thompson opted for a modular approach. They divided the functionality of the operating system into small, self-contained programs called "utilities," each performing a specific task. These utilities could then be combined to create powerful and flexible tools.

Moreover, Unix introduced the concept of a hierarchical file system, where files and directories were organized in a tree-like structure. This design not only made it easier for users to organize their data but also allowed for efficient and intuitive navigation through the system.

One of the most revolutionary aspects of Unix was its emphasis on collaboration and sharing. Ritchie and Thompson envisioned Unix as a system where multiple users could interact and work together simultaneously. They implemented features like time-sharing, which allowed different users to access the system concurrently, and inter-process communication, which enabled processes to exchange data and collaborate.

The creation of the Unix operating system was not without its challenges. The early versions of Unix faced limited resources and technological constraints. Ritchie and Thompson had to make the most of the limited computing power available to them, often resorting to clever optimizations and efficient algorithms.

Additionally, the development of Unix was carried out under the constraints of a research environment. This meant that the system had to be continuously refined and improved to meet the changing needs of the researchers at Bell Labs. It was through this iterative process that Unix evolved into a robust and flexible operating system.

Unix gained popularity both within Bell Labs and in the wider academic community. Its modular design and portability made it an ideal platform for developing and testing new ideas. As a result, many researchers and students started using Unix and contributing their own improvements and software to the system.

In the early 1970s, Bell Labs decided to distribute Unix outside of the organization, marking the beginning of the Unix revolution. The decision to share the source code and allow others to modify and distribute Unix laid the foundation for the open-source movement. This move also allowed Unix to gain widespread adoption and contributed to its rapid evolution.

The impact of Unix on operating systems cannot be overstated. Unix introduced many concepts and techniques that are still in use today, such as multi-user support, file system hierarchies, and a shell-based command-line interface. It also inspired the development of numerous Unix-like systems, including Linux and macOS.

Unix's philosophy of simplicity, modularity, and collaboration continues to influence the design of modern operating systems. Its principles have been embraced by the open-source community, leading to the development of a vast ecosystem of free and open-source software.

As we reflect on the creation of the Unix operating system, we can appreciate the genius of Dennis Ritchie and Ken Thompson. Their vision and dedication gave birth to an operating system that not only transformed computing but also laid the foundation for the open-source movement. The principles and ideas behind Unix continue to inspire and shape the world of technology, reminding us of the enduring legacy of Ritchie's work.

The philosophy of Unix and the UNIX™ trademark

In order to understand the philosophy behind the Unix operating system and its trademark, it is essential to delve into the core principles that guided its development. Unix, created by Dennis Ritchie and Ken Thompson, was born out of a desire for simplicity, flexibility, and collaboration in the world of computing.

Simplicity as the key to elegance

The central tenet of the Unix philosophy is the idea that simplicity leads to elegance and power in software design. The Unix creators believed that a simple and modular approach to building operating systems would result in more robust and efficient software.

Unix embodies this simplicity through its design principles, such as the use of small, independent utilities that can be combined to perform complex tasks. These utilities are designed to do one thing well and can easily communicate with each other through standard interfaces. This approach allows for ease of use, code reusability, and rapid development.

For example, the Unix command-line interface follows the principle of simplicity by providing a concise set of commands that can be combined to perform a wide range of tasks. By keeping the interface simple and consistent, Unix allows users to quickly learn and leverage its power.

Flexibility through modularity

Another key aspect of the Unix philosophy is the emphasis on modularity, which enables flexibility and extensibility in system design. The Unix operating system is composed of small, self-contained components that can be developed and maintained independently.

This modular approach enables system administrators and developers to easily adapt the system to their specific needs. It allows for the seamless integration of new software components, making it possible to add functionality without disrupting the overall system.

Modularity also promotes collaboration by enabling different individuals or teams to work on specific components of the system without interfering with each other. This distributed development model fosters innovation and allows for rapid progress and improvement.

Collaboration and the UNIX™ trademark

The philosophy of Unix extends beyond the technical aspects of software development. It also emphasizes the importance of collaboration and open communication among developers, users, and the broader computing community.

The Unix creators recognized that open collaboration leads to the exchange of ideas, innovation, and collective problem-solving. To facilitate this collaboration, they created a culture of sharing and openness, which laid the foundation for the open-source movement that emerged later.

In fact, the symbol of collaboration in the Unix world is the UNIX™ trademark. The decision to trademark the term "Unix" was a deliberate choice to ensure that all implementations of the system adhered to a set of common principles and standards.

By enforcing the use of the UNIX™ trademark, the creators aimed to protect the integrity, compatibility, and portability of the Unix system. This ensured that users could rely on the same fundamental principles and features across different Unix variants while fostering collaboration and preventing fragmentation.

The power of simplicity, flexibility, and collaboration

The philosophy of Unix and the UNIX™ trademark embody a powerful combination of simplicity, flexibility, and collaboration. These principles have had a profound impact on the world of computing, shaping the development of operating systems, programming languages, and software engineering practices.

The simplicity of Unix has led to its widespread adoption and influenced the design of countless software systems. Its modular and flexible nature has inspired the development of open-source software, enabling innovation and collective problem-solving.

The collaborative spirit fostered by Unix continues to thrive in the modern software industry. Open-source projects, online communities, and collaborative development platforms owe their existence to the principles established by the Unix philosophy.

In conclusion, the philosophy of Unix and the UNIX™ trademark represent a unique approach to software development. Guided by the principles of simplicity, flexibility, and collaboration, Unix has left an indelible mark on the field of computer science, shaping the way software is designed, developed, and shared.

The impact of Unix on operating systems

The birth of Unix in the early 1970s marked a significant turning point in the evolution of operating systems. Developed by Dennis Ritchie and Ken Thompson at Bell Labs, Unix introduced a multitude of innovative concepts that would revolutionize the way operating systems were conceived and implemented. Its impact on the world of operating systems remains unquestionable to this day. In this section, we will explore the profound influence of Unix on operating systems, delving into its key principles, architectural design, and lasting legacy.

The principles of Unix

Unix was built upon a set of fundamental principles that fundamentally transformed the way operating systems were designed and developed. These principles, often referred to as the "Unix philosophy," emphasized simplicity, modularity, and decentralization. The Unix philosophy advocated for minimalist programs that performed specific tasks efficiently, while being easily combined with other programs through a simple and robust interface.

One of the central tenets of the Unix philosophy was the concept of "everything is a file." In Unix, all types of resources, including devices, directories, and processes, were treated as files. This uniformity simplifies the design and implementation of the operating system, allowing for consistent and flexible operations across different resource types.

Furthermore, Unix embraced the idea of "do one thing and do it well." Rather than bundling a myriad of features into a monolithic system, Unix encouraged the development of small, focused programs that excelled in a specific task. These programs could then be easily combined using pipelines, allowing for powerful and flexible data processing workflows.

Architectural design of Unix

The architectural design of Unix played a pivotal role in its impact on operating systems. Unix introduced several key concepts that would shape the future of operating system design, including the notion of a hierarchical file system, process management, and inter-process communication.

One of the most significant contributions of Unix was its hierarchical file system. Unlike previous operating systems, which relied on flat directory structures, Unix organized files and directories in a hierarchical tree-like structure. This allowed for efficient organization and navigation of files and provided a foundation for the implementation of file permissions and user access control.

Unix also introduced a robust process management system. Each running program in Unix was treated as a separate process, with its own address space and execution context. The process management system provided mechanisms for creating, terminating, and communicating between processes, enabling multi-tasking and concurrent execution of programs.

Inter-process communication was another crucial aspect of Unix's architectural design. Unix provided various mechanisms for processes to exchange data and synchronize their actions, including pipes, signals, and shared memory. These mechanisms enabled collaboration and cooperation between processes, fostering the development of complex and distributed applications.

Legacy and influence on modern operating systems

The impact of Unix on operating systems cannot be overstated. Unix introduced a level of elegance and simplicity to operating system design that continues to inspire modern operating systems today. Many key concepts and principles of Unix have been incorporated into numerous operating systems of the past and present, including Linux, macOS, and the various BSD derivatives.

The success of Unix also sparked the rise of the open-source movement in operating systems. Unix's modular and accessible nature made it an ideal candidate for collaborative development, and its source code was shared with academic institutions, leading to the creation of numerous Unix variants. This spirit of openness and collaboration influenced subsequent operating systems, which embraced the idea of freely sharing source code and fostering community-driven development.

Today, the impact of Unix can be observed in the stability, security, and flexibility of modern operating systems. Its design principles, such as modularity and simplicity, have influenced the development of microkernel architectures and containerization technologies. The concepts of hierarchical file systems, process management, and inter-process communication pioneered by Unix are now fundamental components of almost every contemporary operating system.

Challenges and advancements in operating systems

While Unix revolutionized the field of operating systems, it also faced numerous challenges and spurred advancements in subsequent systems. For instance, scalability and performance have always been important concerns in operating system design. As computers became more powerful and capable of handling larger workloads, operating systems had to adapt to effectively utilize available resources.

Another challenge for operating systems lies in providing security and protecting user data. As systems became increasingly interconnected and prone to security threats, operating system designers had to implement robust security mechanisms to safeguard user information and prevent unauthorized access.

Advancements in virtualization and cloud computing have also presented new challenges for operating systems. The ability to run multiple operating system instances concurrently on a single physical machine introduces complexities in resource allocation and isolation. Operating systems must efficiently manage resources and ensure the isolation of different virtual environments.

Moreover, the proliferation of mobile devices and the advent of the Internet of Things (IoT) have necessitated the development of operating systems that are optimized for low-power and resource-constrained environments. These operating systems must strike a delicate balance between functionality and efficiency, providing a seamless user experience while conserving energy and system resources.

In conclusion, Unix's impact on operating systems is far-reaching and long-lasting. Its fundamental principles, architectural design, and lasting legacy have shaped the development of modern operating systems, influencing various aspects such as design philosophy, file systems, process management, and inter-process communication. Unix's emphasis on simplicity, modularity, and decentralization continues to inspire operating system developers, while its open-source heritage has fostered a culture of collaboration and innovation. As operating systems continue to evolve and face new challenges, the lessons learned from Unix remain invaluable in driving progress and ensuring the efficiency and security of future systems.

The growth of the open-source movement

The open-source movement has emerged as a significant force in the software industry, revolutionizing the way software is developed, shared, and distributed. It has its roots in the collaborative and community-oriented ethos of Unix, the operating system developed by Dennis Ritchie and his colleagues at Bell Labs. In this section, we will explore the growth of the open-source movement, its key principles, and the impact it has had on the software industry.

The principles of open source

Open source refers to a development model where the source code of a software program is made freely available for anyone to view, use, modify, and distribute. The open-source movement is built on a set of key principles:

- **Transparency and collaboration:** Open-source projects are developed in a transparent and collaborative manner, with multiple contributors working together to improve the software. This allows for a wide range of perspectives and expertise to come together, resulting in higher-quality software.

- **Licensing:** Open-source software is typically released under licenses that grant users the freedom to use, modify, and distribute the software. These licenses ensure that the software remains open and that any modifications or improvements made by the community are also shared back with the community.

- **Community-driven development:** Open-source projects are driven by communities of developers who share a common interest in the software and its goals. These communities provide support, guidance, and resources to contributors, fostering a sense of belonging and shared responsibility.

- **Continuous improvement:** Open-source software is constantly evolving, with regular updates, bug fixes, and new features being contributed by the community. This continuous improvement ensures that the software remains relevant, secure, and adaptable to changing user needs.

The origins of the open-source movement

The open-source movement can trace its origins back to the Free Software Foundation (FSF) and the GNU Project, launched by Richard Stallman in the

1980s. Stallman's vision was to create a complete operating system composed entirely of free and open-source software.

The development of Unix played a pivotal role in shaping the open-source movement. Unix was developed in a collaborative manner, with multiple programmers contributing their ideas and code. This culture of collaboration and sharing directly influenced the ideals of the open-source movement.

One of the key components of Unix, the C programming language, also played a significant role in the growth of open source. By providing a portable and efficient language for software development, C enabled programmers to develop software that could run on different hardware platforms. This portability made it easier to share and distribute software, laying the foundation for the open-source movement.

The rise of Linux

The open-source' movement gained significant momentum with the release of the Linux operating system in 1991 by Linus Torvalds. Linux was built on the principles of open source, with its source code made freely available to the public. It quickly gathered a dedicated community of developers who contributed their skills and expertise to improve the system.

Linux emerged as a powerful and versatile alternative to proprietary operating systems like Windows and Unix. Its open nature allowed for rapid development and innovation, attracting both individual developers and major companies who saw the potential of an open-source operating system.

The success of Linux demonstrated the viability and benefits of the open-source model. It provided a powerful platform for developers to collaborate and innovate, resulting in a robust and stable operating system that could compete with proprietary alternatives.

The impact of open source on the software industry

The growth of the open-source movement has had a profound impact on the software industry. It has challenged the traditional business models built around proprietary software and introduced new ways of developing and distributing software. Some key impacts include:

- **Increased innovation:** The open-source model encourages innovation by allowing developers to freely experiment, modify, and improve upon existing software. This has led to the creation of a vast ecosystem of open-source projects and libraries that serve as building blocks for new software development.

+ **Cost savings:** Open-source software is often available free of charge, which has resulted in significant cost savings for individuals and organizations. This accessibility has democratized access to high-quality software, leveling the playing field for smaller businesses and promoting digital inclusion.

+ **Security and reliability:** Open-source software is subject to peer review and scrutiny by a large community of developers, which enhances security and reliability. Vulnerabilities and bugs can be quickly identified and fixed, leading to more robust and secure software.

+ **Fostering collaboration and knowledge sharing:** The open-source model promotes collaboration and knowledge sharing among developers. It fosters a culture of transparency, encourages the exchange of ideas and best practices, and facilitates the collective growth of the software development community.

+ **Driving interoperability and standardization:** Open-source software often adheres to open standards, promoting interoperability between different systems and software. This helps to prevent vendor lock-in and allows for greater flexibility and choice for users.

Challenges and future directions

While the open-source movement has achieved remarkable success, it also faces several challenges. Some of these challenges include:

+ **Sustainability:** Open-source projects often rely on volunteer contributions, making sustainability a significant concern. Finding sustainable funding models and ensuring ongoing support and maintenance is crucial for the long-term success of open-source software.

+ **Fragmentation:** The decentralized nature of open-source development can lead to fragmentation, with multiple competing versions of software and incompatible standards. Overcoming fragmentation requires effective communication, coordination, and governance within open-source communities.

+ **Legal and licensing issues:** Open-source software must navigate complex legal and licensing issues. Ensuring compliance with licenses, managing intellectual property, and addressing copyright and patent concerns are ongoing challenges for open-source projects.

Looking to the future, the open-source movement is likely to continue its growth and influence. With the increasing reliance on software in various domains, the principles of openness, collaboration, and transparency offered by open source will remain attractive to developers and users alike. The open-source movement will play a vital role in shaping the future of the software industry, driving innovation, and enabling the development of robust and secure software systems. As developers and users, we have a responsibility to support and contribute to the open-source community, ensuring its continued success and impact.

Ritchie's role in the development of open-source software

The concept of open-source software has revolutionized the way programmers collaborate and build software. One of the key figures in the development of open-source software is Dennis Ritchie, who played a crucial role in shaping this movement.

2.2.5.1 Early Encounters with Open-source

Dennis Ritchie's journey into the world of open-source began with the creation of the Unix operating system. Unix was developed as a collaborative effort between Ritchie and his colleague Ken Thompson at Bell Labs in the late 1960s. Unlike proprietary software at the time, Unix was designed to be freely shared and enhanced by the programming community.

2.2.5.2 Unix Philosophy and the Birth of a Movement

The philosophy behind Unix was rooted in simplicity, elegance, and openness. Through Ritchie's meticulous design and Thompson's implementation, they created an operating system that was modular, flexible, and customizable. The fundamental principles of Unix included:

1. The "do one thing and do it well" principle: This concept emphasized the development of small, focused software components that performed specific tasks efficiently. Each component was designed to communicate with other components through a simple and standardized interface.

2. The use of plain text for data interchange: Unix adopted the convention of representing data using plain text, which made it easy to read, manipulate, and transfer information between different programs. This principle promoted interoperability and facilitated collaboration.

3. The emphasis on "software tools": Unix introduced the concept of small, specialized programs called "software tools" that could be combined in various ways to accomplish complex tasks. These tools were designed to be reusable, allowing programmers to create powerful solutions by leveraging existing components.

The success of Unix and its philosophy laid the foundation for the open-source movement. The collaborative culture and the concept of freely sharing software made Unix an ideal platform for developers to contribute and improve upon the system.

2.2.5.3 The Evolution of Open-source Software

Ritchie's role in the development of open-source software extended beyond the creation of Unix. As Unix gained popularity, more developers began to contribute their enhancements and bug fixes to the system. Ritchie played a pivotal role in managing these contributions and incorporating them into the official Unix releases.

Ritchie also actively participated in the broader open-source community. He joined forces with other prominent programmers, such as Richard Stallman, to advocate for the sharing of source code and the freedom to modify and distribute software. Together, they laid the groundwork for the free software movement and the creation of the GNU Project, which aimed to develop a complete and free Unix-like operating system.

2.2.5.4 The Impact of Ritchie's Contributions

Ritchie's contributions to the development of open-source software had a profound impact on the software industry and the programming community. Here are some key aspects of his role:

1. Enabling collaboration and innovation: By fostering a culture of collaboration, Ritchie paved the way for programmers worldwide to contribute their ideas and improvements to Unix. This collaborative environment fueled rapid innovation, allowing Unix to evolve and adapt to the changing needs of users.

2. Advancing the principles of open-source: Ritchie's commitment to open-source software and his advocacy for the sharing of code influenced subsequent projects, including the development of the GNU/Linux operating system. His ideas provided a philosophical foundation for the open-source movement, promoting transparency, freedom, and community engagement.

3. Inspiring future generations of programmers: Through his work on Unix and open-source software, Ritchie inspired countless programmers to adopt a collaborative and open approach to software development. The values and principles he championed continue to shape the mindset of developers today, fostering a spirit of sharing and cooperation.

2.2.5.5 Challenges and Lessons Learned

Ritchie faced several challenges during his journey in open-source software development. One major challenge was managing the diverse contributions from the community while ensuring the stability and reliability of the Unix system. Ritchie and his team developed robust processes to evaluate and integrate these contributions, ensuring that the system remained cohesive and secure.

Another challenge was balancing the need for innovation with the practicality of software design. Ritchie believed in creating elegant and efficient solutions, but he also recognized the importance of practicality and usability. The Unix system, with its focus on simplicity and compatibility, served as a testament to Ritchie's ability to strike this delicate balance.

From Ritchie's experiences, we can learn valuable lessons in open-source software development. Collaboration and community involvement are essential for sustained improvement and innovation. Encouraging transparent communication channels and creating structured processes for evaluating and integrating contributions help maintain the integrity of the project. Balancing innovation and practicality ensures that software remains usable and relevant, without sacrificing creativity.

2.2.5.6 Future of Open-source and Ritchie's Enduring Legacy

Ritchie's contributions to open-source software continue to shape the future of software development. The principles of collaboration, transparency, and community-driven innovation that he advocated for are now deeply ingrained in the DNA of the open-source movement.

As the software industry evolves, the lessons learned from Ritchie's experiences remain relevant. Open-source software has become a powerful force in the modern world, powering critical infrastructure, driving technological advancements, and empowering developers worldwide.

To honor Ritchie's enduring legacy, it is crucial for industry leaders, programmers, and educators to continue building upon his ideas. By embracing open-source practices, supporting community-driven initiatives, and preserving the principles of collaboration and innovation, we can ensure the longevity of Ritchie's contributions and pave the way for a vibrant and sustainable future in software development.

Awards, honors, and recognition

The Turing Award and its significance

The Turing Award, often referred to as the "Nobel Prize of computing," is an annual prize given by the Association for Computing Machinery (ACM) to individuals who have made significant contributions to the field of computer science. Named after the renowned British mathematician and computer scientist Alan Turing, the award was established in 1966 to recognize and honor groundbreaking achievements in computer science.

The significance of the Turing Award goes beyond mere recognition. It serves as an acknowledgment of extraordinary talent and creativity in the field of computing, and it symbolizes the highest level of achievement in computer science. The recipients of this prestigious award have not only made groundbreaking contributions to their respective research areas but have also demonstrated exceptional vision, innovation, and impact on the discipline as a whole.

The Turing Award is given for specific technical contributions that have fundamentally advanced the field of computer science. The ACM recognizes contributions in a wide range of areas within computer science, including algorithms and data structures, programming languages, software engineering, computer architecture, artificial intelligence, and human-computer interaction, among others.

The recipients of the Turing Award have made significant contributions to various areas of computer science, each pushing the boundaries of knowledge and technology in their respective fields. Some notable recipients include Donald Knuth for his pioneering work in algorithms and typesetting systems, Edsger Dijkstra for his fundamental contributions to programming languages and algorithms, and John McCarthy for his role in the development of artificial intelligence and the Lisp programming language.

The Turing Award not only acknowledges and rewards the exceptional work of individuals but also raises awareness of their contributions among the wider public. It highlights the importance of their research and its impact on society, inspiring future generations of computer scientists to push the boundaries of knowledge and drive technological innovation.

To date, the Turing Award has recognized the achievements of computer scientists from around the world, emphasizing the global nature of the field and the universal impact of their research. This award has become a symbol of excellence in computer science, and its recipients are seen as trailblazers and visionaries who have transformed the way we think about and interact with technology.

It is important to note that the significance of the Turing Award extends beyond the recognition it bestows on its recipients. It serves as a reminder of the immense potential and power of computer science to shape and improve our world. By honoring those who have made exceptional contributions to the discipline, the Turing Award inspires future generations to pursue their own groundbreaking research and continue the legacy of innovation and progress.

In conclusion, the Turing Award is a highly esteemed recognition in the field of computer science, honoring individuals who have made extraordinary contributions to the discipline. It serves as a testament to the importance of their work and its impact on society. By celebrating the achievements of these exceptional individuals, the Turing Award inspires future generations to strive for excellence and make their mark on the ever-evolving field of computer science.

Other prestigious awards and accolades received by Ritchie

Dennis Ritchie, a true pioneer and genius in the world of computer science, received numerous prestigious awards and accolades throughout his career. These honors recognized his groundbreaking contributions to programming languages, operating systems, and the software industry as a whole. Let's take a closer look at some of the significant awards and recognition that Ritchie received.

The National Medal of Technology and Innovation

In 1998, Dennis Ritchie was awarded the National Medal of Technology and Innovation by the United States government. This highly esteemed honor is awarded annually to individuals who have made significant contributions to the advancement of technology and have had a substantial impact on the nation's economic, environmental, and social well-being. Ritchie's pioneering work in the development of the C language and Unix operating system made him a worthy recipient of this prestigious award.

The IEEE Richard W. Hamming Medal

In 1990, the Institute of Electrical and Electronics Engineers (IEEE) awarded Ritchie the Richard W. Hamming Medal. This award is bestowed upon individuals who have made exceptional contributions to information sciences, systems, and technologies. Ritchie's influential work in the field of programming languages, particularly the development of the C language, made him a natural choice for this esteemed recognition.

The Turning Award: The Highest Honor in Computer Science

No discussion of Dennis Ritchie's accolades would be complete without mentioning the most prestigious award in the field of computer science: the Turing Award. In 1983, Ritchie, alongside his collaborator Ken Thompson, was awarded the Turing Award by the Association for Computing Machinery (ACM). The Turing Award is often referred to as the "Nobel Prize of Computing" and is given to individuals who have made lasting and substantial contributions to the field. Ritchie and Thompson were recognized for their creation of the Unix operating system and the development of the C programming language, which revolutionized the field of software development.

The Japan Prize

The Japan Prize is an international award presented to individuals who have made significant advancements in the fields of science, technology, and society. In 2011, Dennis Ritchie was honored with the Japan Prize for his exceptional contributions to the development of the C language and the Unix operating system. This award not only recognized Ritchie's technical accomplishments but also highlighted the global impact of his work.

Other Notable Accolades

In addition to the above-mentioned awards, Dennis Ritchie received many other notable accolades throughout his career. These include the ACM Software System Award, the ACM Grace Murray Hopper Award, and the IEEE John von Neumann Medal, among others. Each of these awards recognized Ritchie's outstanding contributions to computer science and solidified his status as one of the most influential figures in the field.

Legacy and Impact

The numerous awards and accolades received by Dennis Ritchie underscore the profound impact he had on computer science and the software industry. His groundbreaking work in the development of the C language and Unix operating system revolutionized the field of programming and paved the way for future innovations. Ritchie's legacy lives on through the millions of programmers whose lives have been touched by his creations and through the ongoing relevance and importance of the C language. It is imperative that we continue to honor Ritchie's memory and preserve his work for future generations of programmers to learn from and build upon.

Recognition and influence within the programming community

Dennis Ritchie's contributions to the programming community cannot be overstated. Throughout his career, he received recognition and earned profound respect from his peers for his groundbreaking work in the development of the C language and the Unix operating system. Let us explore the recognition and influence he received within the programming community.

The C language and its impact

One of Dennis Ritchie's greatest achievements was the creation of the C programming language. From its inception, the C language gained immense popularity and quickly became a dominant force in the programming world. Its simplicity, efficiency, and portability revolutionized software development and influenced a generation of programmers.

Developers worldwide recognized the power and versatility of the C language. Its ability to write low-level code while maintaining a high-level approach made it an ideal choice for many applications. As a result, C became the language of choice for operating systems and embedded systems.

The influence of the C language can be witnessed in numerous programming languages that exist today. Languages like C++, C#, Java, and Objective-C have borrowed heavily from the syntax and structure of C. This influence can be attributed to Dennis Ritchie's pioneering work in creating a language that was both expressive and efficient.

Industry recognition

Dennis Ritchie's contributions to the field of programming were widely recognized by industry leaders and organizations. In 1983, he was awarded the Turing Award, considered the highest honor in computer science. The award acknowledged his role in the development of the C language and the impact it had on computer systems.

Beyond the Turing Award, Ritchie received various accolades throughout his career. He was elected to the National Academy of Engineering in 1988 for his contributions to software engineering. His work also earned him the IEEE Richard W. Hamming Medal in 1990, further solidifying his position as a pioneer in the field.

Ritchie's recognition extended beyond formal awards. He became a highly sought-after speaker and participated in numerous conferences and seminars, where he shared his insights and experiences with fellow programmers. His reputation as a visionary and a programming luminary grew with each passing year.

Influence on future generations

Dennis Ritchie's influence continues to resonate within the programming community, even after his passing. His work on the C language and the Unix operating system laid the foundation for modern computing. The concepts and principles he established shaped the way we build software today.

Many programmers credit Ritchie's innovations as instrumental in shaping their careers. His approach to programming, emphasizing simplicity and elegance, has been a guiding light for aspiring programmers. The widespread adoption of the C language means that his influence can be felt in a vast array of fields and applications.

Ritchie's work also left a lasting impact on programming culture. His dedication to collaboration and teamwork fostered a spirit of community within the programming community. The open-source movement, which grew in parallel with the development of Unix, owes a debt of gratitude to Ritchie for his role in fostering a culture of sharing and openness.

Preserving Ritchie's legacy

The programming community recognizes the importance of preserving Dennis Ritchie's work and memory. Despite his immense contributions, Ritchie remained a humble and unassuming individual. To honor his legacy, efforts have been made to document and preserve his code, papers, and other artifacts.

The ongoing development and support for the C language ensure that Ritchie's ideas and concepts live on. The C language continues to be taught in universities and used by professionals around the world. The dedication to maintaining the simplicity and elegance of the language carries forward Ritchie's spirit of innovation.

In conclusion, Dennis Ritchie's recognition and influence within the programming community are undeniable. His creation of the C language and his work on Unix revolutionized software development. The impact of his ideas and concepts will continue to shape the field of programming for generations to come. It is our responsibility, as programmers, to carry on his legacy by embracing his principles of simplicity, collaboration, and innovation.

Legacy and impact on future generations of programmers

Dennis Ritchie's contributions to the field of computer science have left a lasting legacy, greatly impacting and influencing future generations of programmers. His work on the development of the C language and Unix operating system has shaped the foundation of modern programming and software development. In this section, we will explore the lasting legacy of Dennis Ritchie and the profound impact he has had on the programming community.

The C language as a timeless foundation

One of Ritchie's most significant contributions was the creation of the C programming language. C revolutionized the programming landscape by providing a simple yet powerful tool for software development. Its elegant syntax and efficient design made it accessible to both novice and expert programmers, establishing it as a timeless foundation for various domains of programming.

The C language's influence can be seen in numerous modern programming languages, including C++, Java, and C#. The concepts and principles introduced by Ritchie, such as procedural programming and structured programming, have become fundamental pillars of software development.

C's influence extends beyond its direct descendants, as it continues to inspire and shape the design of new programming languages. Its emphasis on efficiency, portability, and low-level control has made it a preferred choice for systems programming and embedded systems development.

A mindset of innovation and collaboration

Ritchie's legacy extends beyond his technical contributions; he also left an indelible mark on the programming culture. He fostered a mindset of innovation and collaboration that continues to inspire programmers to push the boundaries of what is possible.

Ritchie believed in the power of teamwork and collaboration, as exemplified by his partnership with Ken Thompson during the development of Unix. Their work on Unix demonstrated the potential of collective creativity and sparked the open-source movement, enabling programmers worldwide to collaborate and contribute to the advancement of software.

His approach to problem-solving encouraged programmers to think outside the box and embrace unconventional solutions. Ritchie's willingness to challenge existing norms and conventions pushed the boundaries of what was considered possible in software development.

Preserving Ritchie's spirit

As future generations of programmers carry the torch forward, it is essential to preserve and honor Dennis Ritchie's legacy. This involves not only leveraging the concepts and principles he introduced but also embodying the spirit of innovation, collaboration, and curiosity that he exemplified.

Programmers must continue to build upon Ritchie's ideas, adapting and evolving them to address the ever-changing demands of the software industry. By embracing the principles of simplicity, efficiency, and portability that underpin the C language, programmers can create robust and reliable software that stands the test of time.

Furthermore, the importance of understanding programming history cannot be overstated. By studying Ritchie's work and the development of the C language, programmers gain insights into both the evolution of programming languages and the underlying principles that continue to shape the field.

Challenges and future possibilities

While Ritchie's contributions have had a profound impact on the field of computer science, future generations of programmers face new challenges and opportunities. As technology continues to advance, programming languages and paradigms must keep pace with evolving requirements.

Consequently, programmers must strike a balance between preserving the core principles and concepts established by Ritchie while embracing innovation and new approaches. This necessitates staying informed about emerging technologies, frameworks, and programming methodologies, while keeping sight of the significant contributions that paved the way.

The future possibilities for programmers are seemingly limitless. From artificial intelligence and machine learning to quantum computing and cyber-physical systems, the expanding frontier of computer science offers programmers unprecedented opportunities to make significant contributions and shape the future.

Carrying on Ritchie's legacy

Ultimately, the responsibility lies with programmers to carry on the legacy of Dennis Ritchie. By embracing his spirit of innovation, collaboration, and relentless pursuit of excellence, programmers can continue to push the boundaries of what is possible and drive the field of computer science forward.

It is crucial to recognize and celebrate Ritchie's contributions, both by incorporating his principles into our work and by educating future generations about his invaluable contributions to the field. By doing so, we ensure that his legacy lives on and continues to inspire and guide programmers for years to come.

Summary

Dennis Ritchie's impact on future generations of programmers is immeasurable. His creation of the C language and his contributions to the development of Unix have shaped the foundation of modern programming. By embracing Ritchie's principles of simplicity, efficiency, and collaboration, programmers can continue to build upon his legacy and drive the field of computer science forward. The possibilities for future innovations are vast, and by carrying on Ritchie's spirit of innovation and excellence, programmers can contribute to the evolving landscape of software development.

The importance of preserving Ritchie's work and memory

Preserving the work and memory of Dennis Ritchie is of paramount importance in the field of computer science. As the pioneer of the C programming language and a key figure in the development of the Unix operating system, Ritchie's contributions have had a lasting impact on the world of software development.

Preserving Ritchie's work

Ritchie's work laid the foundation for modern programming languages and operating systems. The C programming language, with its simplicity, efficiency, and portability, revolutionized the software industry. It became the preferred language for writing systems software, embedded systems, and even applications. It directly influenced the development of languages like C++, Objective-C, and C#.

Preserving Ritchie's work entails ensuring that the C language remains accessible and well-documented for future generations of programmers. This includes maintaining and updating the C language standards, providing comprehensive documentation, and supporting compilers and development tools. By doing so, we can ensure that Ritchie's ideas and concepts continue to be used and innovated upon.

Furthermore, it is crucial to preserve Ritchie's work by nurturing a culture of open-source development. Many of Ritchie's projects, including the Unix operating system, were developed collaboratively and released as open-source software. By embracing openness and collaboration, we can honor Ritchie's legacy and foster the development of high-quality, community-driven projects.

Preserving Ritchie's memory

Preserving Ritchie's memory is essential not only for acknowledging his contributions but also for inspiring future generations of programmers. Ritchie's achievements serve as a reminder of the transformative power of innovation, collaboration, and perseverance.

One way to preserve Ritchie's memory is through educational initiatives. Incorporating Ritchie's work into computer science curricula ensures that students learn about his contributions and understand the fundamental concepts of programming languages and operating systems. By studying Ritchie's ideas, students can gain a deeper understanding of the evolution of computer science and appreciate the principles that underpin modern software development.

Another way to honor Ritchie's memory is by commemorating his work and promoting his legacy in the programming community. Establishing scholarships, awards, and conferences in his name can encourage continued research and innovation in the areas that Ritchie pioneered. These initiatives also serve as a platform for programmers to come together, share ideas, and collaborate on projects that extend Ritchie's work.

Additionally, it is important to document stories and anecdotes about Ritchie's life and work. These personal accounts provide a window into the man behind the code and help us understand the motivations, challenges, and triumphs he faced throughout his career. Preserving Ritchie's memory in this way humanizes his accomplishments and ensures that he is remembered not just as a brilliant programmer, but as a person who made a profound impact on the world of computing.

The future of preserving Ritchie's work and memory

Preserving Ritchie's work and memory requires ongoing commitment and effort. As technology evolves, it is crucial to adapt and update the tools, standards, and documentation related to the C language. This ensures that the language remains relevant and continues to be a powerful tool for software development.

Furthermore, collaboration between industry leaders, educational institutions, and the open-source community is essential. By working together, we can ensure that Ritchie's ideas and principles are not lost to time but continue to shape and inspire future generations of programmers.

In conclusion, preserving the work and memory of Dennis Ritchie is vital for honoring his contributions, understanding the foundations of programming languages and operating systems, and inspiring future innovations. By preserving

Ritchie's work through maintaining the C language and nurturing open-source development, and by commemorating his memory through education and community initiatives, we can ensure that his legacy lives on, shaping the future of computer science.

Chapter Three: Behind the Scenes

The personal life of Dennis Ritchie

Relationships and Friendships

In the realm of computer science, Dennis Ritchie was not only known for his groundbreaking contributions but also for the deep connections he forged with fellow programmers and colleagues. Despite his quiet and introverted nature, Ritchie had a profound impact on those who had the opportunity to work alongside him, both professionally and personally. This section explores the relationships and friendships that shaped Ritchie's life and career, highlighting the important role they played in his journey.

Friendship with Ken Thompson

One of the most significant relationships in Dennis Ritchie's life was his friendship and collaboration with Ken Thompson. Ritchie and Thompson first met while working at Bell Labs, where they embarked on a journey to develop the Unix operating system. This partnership would prove to be one of the most influential in the history of computer science.

Ritchie and Thompson shared a common vision for Unix and worked in close tandem to bring that vision to life. Their friendship extended beyond the professional realm, as they often spent time together outside of work. They would frequently engage in discussions about computing, exchange ideas, and challenge each other's perspectives. This intense collaboration and camaraderie allowed them to push the boundaries of what was thought possible in the field of operating systems.

The deep trust and mutual respect between Ritchie and Thompson were evident in their work on the C programming language. Ritchie's expertise in language design and Thompson's insights into system programming resulted in a language that was not only elegant and efficient but also perfectly suited for the needs of Unix. Their close bond played a crucial role in the rapid advancement and success of both Unix and the C language.

Collaboration at Bell Labs

Beyond his friendship with Thompson, Dennis Ritchie had a profound impact on the culture of collaboration at Bell Labs. Despite being an inherently introverted person, Ritchie recognized the value of collaboration within the programming community. He actively sought opportunities to collaborate with his colleagues, ensuring that knowledge and expertise were shared freely.

Ritchie's collaborative approach extended to the mentorship of younger programmers, and he would often take the time to guide and support them in their work. This nurturing spirit created a sense of community among the programmers at Bell Labs, fostering an environment where ideas could flourish and innovations could take shape.

Ritchie's collaborative nature was also evident in his involvement in various standards committees, where he worked with other prominent programmers in the industry. Through these collaborations, Ritchie contributed to the standardization efforts of programming languages and software development practices, leaving a lasting impact on the field.

Professional Network

Dennis Ritchie's influence extended far beyond his immediate circle of friends and colleagues. Throughout his career, he connected with numerous programmers and computer scientists, building a robust professional network that spanned the globe.

Ritchie actively participated in conferences, seminars, and workshops, where he would share his knowledge and engage in discussions with fellow experts. These events served as opportunities for him to expand his network and learn from others in the field. The connections he made during these interactions further enriched his work and informed his contributions to the programming community.

Ritchie's willingness to connect and collaborate with professionals from diverse backgrounds allowed him to tap into a wealth of ideas and perspectives. It also ensured that his work continued to evolve, drawing inspiration from a wide range of sources.

Personal Bonds

Beyond his professional relationships, Dennis Ritchie valued and nurtured personal bonds with those closest to him. Although known for his dedication to his work, Ritchie recognized the importance of maintaining a balance between his personal and professional life.

He valued his relationships with family and friends, who provided him with a sense of support and grounding. Spending time with loved ones allowed him to relax and recharge, nurturing his creativity and passion for programming.

Ritchie's personal connections served as a reminder that the impact of one's work goes beyond professional achievements. These relationships played a significant role in shaping his character and influencing his approach to programming and life as a whole.

Conclusion

In this section, we explored the relationships and friendships that were integral to Dennis Ritchie's life and career. This examination revealed the profound impact these connections had on his journey as a programmer and innovator.

From his close friendship and collaboration with Ken Thompson to his commitment to fostering a culture of collaboration at Bell Labs, Ritchie recognized the power of working together and exchanging ideas. His personal and professional relationships, coupled with his innate curiosity and perseverance, allowed him to push the boundaries of computer science.

Ritchie's emphasis on relationships serves as a reminder that innovation does not happen in isolation. Meaningful connections and collaborations are the catalysts that drive progress and change. As we celebrate Dennis Ritchie's contributions, it is essential to recognize and cultivate the power of relationships in our own journeys as programmers and researchers. By doing so, we can pay homage to the legacy of Dennis Ritchie and ensure a bright future for the field of computer science.

Hobbies and interests outside of programming

Dennis Ritchie's life was not solely defined by his relentless dedication to programming and technological pursuits. Outside of the world of coding, Ritchie had a diverse range of hobbies and interests that added depth to his personality and helped shape his innovative mindset.

One of Ritchie's primary passions outside of programming was music. He had a deep appreciation for classical music, which he often found intellectually stimulating and spiritually uplifting. Ritchie particularly enjoyed attending live orchestra performances and would frequently immerse himself in the symphonies and concertos of composers like Beethoven, Mozart, and Bach. He found solace in the harmonies and melodies that transcended the boundaries of programming and allowed his mind to wander into a different realm of creativity.

In addition to his love for classical music, Ritchie was a skilled amateur pianist. He would spend hours improvising and composing his own music on the piano, using it as a means to express and explore his emotions. Music provided him with a sense of release and rejuvenation, allowing him to approach programming with a fresh perspective.

Ritchie also had an affinity for literature, often losing himself in the pages of novels and poetry. He was captivated by the power of words and the ability of writers to convey complex emotions and ideas. As an avid reader, Ritchie's literary interests spanned various genres, with a particular fondness for science fiction and philosophical works. He believed that literature had the potential to ignite the imagination and inspire groundbreaking ideas, even in the realm of programming.

Another interest that Ritchie nurtured outside of programming was photography. He found joy in capturing moments and scenes that caught his eye, often experimenting with different techniques and perspectives. Ritchie believed that photography allowed him to view the world from a different lens, helping him refine his observational skills and attention to detail. Being behind the camera gave him a sense of peace and allowed him to observe the beauty in the simplest of things, enabling him to bring a different perspective to the complexities of programming.

Ritchie appreciated the great outdoors and embraced nature as a source of inspiration. He found solace in taking long walks, exploring forests, and observing the wonders of the natural world. This connection to nature served as a reminder of the vastness of the universe and the importance of preserving and understanding our place within it. Ritchie believed that spending time in nature fostered a sense of humility and helped him appreciate the intricate complexities of the world, which he could then bring into his programming endeavors.

Interestingly, Ritchie also had a fascination with puzzles and games. He enjoyed challenging his mind with mathematical problems, riddles, and brain teasers. This love for puzzles not only provided entertainment and a means to unwind, but also sharpened his analytical and problem-solving skills. Ritchie understood the importance of thinking outside the box and engaging in activities that stretched his mental boundaries, as it fostered a creative and innovative mindset that he then applied to his programming projects.

In conclusion, Dennis Ritchie was not solely defined by his contributions to the world of programming. Outside of his programming pursuits, Ritchie had diverse interests that ranged from music and literature to photography and nature. These hobbies and interests served as outlets for his creative energy, fostering a well-rounded mindset that ultimately enriched his programming endeavors. Ritchie's unconventional approach to programming, inspired by his varied interests, continues to inspire aspiring programmers to think beyond the confines of code and explore the world around them for inspiration and innovative solutions.

Personal quirks and habits

Dennis Ritchie, although a programming genius, was not immune to the idiosyncrasies that make us all unique. He had his fair share of personal quirks and habits that shaped his work and daily life. These quirks, though seemingly trivial, provide insight into the mind of a brilliant programmer.

Coffee addiction and late-night coding sessions

One of Ritchie's most well-known personal habits was his addiction to coffee. He was often seen with a cup of coffee in hand, which fueled his late-night coding sessions. Ritchie believed that caffeine helped him stay focused and alert during the long hours he spent writing code. He would often work late into the night, fueled by his love for programming and the stimulating effects of coffee.

Obsession with perfection and attention to detail

Ritchie was known for his obsession with perfection and his meticulous attention to detail. He would spend hours fine-tuning his code, ensuring that every line was written with precision. He believed that the smallest details could have a significant impact on the overall performance and reliability of a program. This attention to detail became one of Ritchie's defining traits, setting him apart as a programmer and engineer.

Love for simplicity and elegance

Despite his intricate attention to detail, Ritchie had a deep appreciation for simplicity and elegance in his code. He believed that a programming language should be easy to understand, allowing programmers to write efficient and clear code. This philosophy was reflected in the design of the C language, which prioritized simplicity and minimalism. Ritchie's love for simplicity guided his approach to problem-solving and software development.

Quiet and reserved nature

Ritchie was known for his quiet and reserved nature. He didn't seek the limelight or crave attention for his accomplishments. Instead, he found solace in his work, often preferring the company of computers over people. This introverted personality allowed Ritchie to channel his energies into his programming endeavors, leading to groundbreaking innovations in the field of computer science.

Disciplined work ethic and focus

Ritchie's disciplined work ethic played a significant role in his success as a programmer. He maintained a structured schedule, dedicating uninterrupted time to his work. He believed in the power of deep focus and concentrated effort, allowing him to tackle complex problems and write code efficiently. Ritchie's disciplined work ethic set an example for future generations of programmers, demonstrating the value of dedication and perseverance.

Fondness for puzzles and problem-solving

Outside of his professional life, Ritchie had a fondness for puzzles and problem-solving. He enjoyed challenging his mind with intricate puzzles and puzzles that required logical thinking. This passion for problem-solving likely contributed to his ability to develop innovative solutions and think outside the box when faced with programming challenges.

Embracing a minimalist lifestyle

Ritchie lived a minimalist lifestyle, reflecting his love for simplicity in all aspects of his life. He believed in the importance of decluttering and only keeping the essentials. This minimalist approach extended to his workspace, where he maintained a clean and organized environment. Ritchie's minimalist lifestyle allowed him to focus his energy on his work and eliminate distractions.

Devotion to continuous learning

Throughout his life, Ritchie maintained a deep devotion to continuous learning. He was always eager to explore new technologies, programming languages, and methodologies. He believed that staying current with the latest advancements in the field was essential for innovation and growth. Ritchie's commitment to continuous learning serves as an inspiration to programmers to never stop seeking knowledge and expanding their horizons.

In conclusion, Dennis Ritchie's personal quirks and habits reveal a unique blend of passion, discipline, and creativity. From his coffee addiction and late-night coding sessions to his obsession with perfection and simplicity, each quirk contributed to his success as a programmer. Ritchie's personal traits remind us of the importance of focus, continuous learning, and embracing our individuality in the pursuit of excellence.

Ritchie's approach to work-life balance

In the fast-paced world of computer programming, finding a healthy work-life balance can be challenging. However, Dennis Ritchie, the brilliant mind behind the C programming language, understood the importance of maintaining a well-rounded life beyond his innovative work. Let's explore Ritchie's approach to work-life balance and the valuable lessons we can learn from his example.

The value of time management

Ritchie recognized that effective time management was essential for achieving work-life balance. He understood that programming required intense focus and concentration, but he also knew the importance of taking breaks and giving himself time for personal activities. Ritchie employed various techniques to manage his time efficiently, allowing him to excel in both his professional and personal endeavors.

One of Ritchie's time management strategies was the use of a structured work routine. He would divide his workday into dedicated blocks of time, during which he focused solely on coding and problem-solving. By setting aside specific hours for work, Ritchie ensured that he could fully immerse himself in his programming tasks without distractions or interruptions.

Additionally, Ritchie understood the significance of prioritization. He would create a to-do list, outlining the most important tasks for the day. By prioritizing his work, Ritchie ensured that he allocated sufficient time to critical projects, while also leaving space for personal interests and hobbies.

Nurturing personal interests

Despite his immense dedication to programming, Ritchie realized the importance of cultivating personal interests outside of his professional life. He recognized that engaging in activities outside of work allowed him to recharge and find inspiration, ultimately enhancing his creativity and problem-solving abilities.

One of Ritchie's favorite hobbies was playing the guitar. He would spend time practicing and exploring different musical genres. This creative outlet not only provided a much-needed break from the complexities of programming but also allowed Ritchie to exercise a different part of his brain. Many programmers find solace in artistic pursuits, as it offers a contrast to the analytical thinking required in coding.

Ritchie also enjoyed spending time outdoors and connecting with nature. He would frequently go for long walks, appreciating the beauty of the natural world.

This helped him relax, clear his mind, and foster a sense of tranquility amidst the demands of his work.

Maintaining relationships

While Ritchie dedicated himself to his work, he understood that fostering meaningful relationships was equally important. He valued the support and companionship of family, friends, and colleagues, recognizing that nurturing these connections played a vital role in his overall well-being.

Ritchie made a conscious effort to spend quality time with his loved ones. He would prioritize family gatherings, social events, and celebrations, ensuring that he was present and engaged. By disconnecting from work during these moments, Ritchie strengthened his relationships and found fulfillment outside of his professional achievements.

Furthermore, Ritchie believed in the power of collaboration and teamwork. He created a culture of collaboration at Bell Labs, encouraging open communication, idea sharing, and mutual support among his colleagues. This collaborative environment not only fostered innovation but also emphasized the importance of maintaining a healthy work-life balance.

The significance of self-care

In addition to his time management strategies, personal interests, and relationships, Ritchie understood the importance of self-care. He recognized that taking care of his physical and mental well-being was crucial for sustained productivity and overall happiness.

Ritchie prioritized regular exercise, ensuring that he incorporated physical activity into his routine. Whether it was going for a run, practicing yoga, or taking part in other fitness activities, he understood the benefits of staying active. Physical exercise not only boosted his energy levels but also relieved stress and enhanced his cognitive abilities.

Moreover, Ritchie made it a priority to get enough rest and sleep. He understood that a well-rested mind was essential for optimal productivity and creativity. By ensuring he got sufficient sleep each night, Ritchie was able to approach his work with focus and clarity.

Lessons learned from Ritchie's approach

Ritchie's approach to work-life balance teaches us valuable lessons that can be applied to our own lives as programmers or individuals in any field. By embracing effective time management, nurturing personal interests, prioritizing relationships, and practicing self-care, we can achieve a healthier and more fulfilling work-life balance.

Finding a balance between our professional and personal lives not only enhances our well-being but also boosts our productivity and creativity in the long run. Let Dennis Ritchie's example inspire us to take a step back from our work, explore our passions, connect with others, and prioritize self-care. In doing so, we can lead happier, more fulfilling lives while continuing to make valuable contributions in our chosen fields.

The impact of personal experiences on Ritchie's work

Dennis Ritchie's personal experiences played a significant role in shaping his work as a programmer and a pioneer in computer science. His upbringing, education, and personal interests all contributed to his unique perspective and approach to programming. In this section, we will explore some of the key personal experiences that influenced Ritchie's work and the lasting impact they had on the field of computer science.

1. Early exposure to technology

Ritchie's first encounters with computers during his childhood had a profound impact on his career. Growing up in a technologically inclined family, he was exposed to various electronic gadgets and devices from an early age. This exposure sparked his curiosity and fascination with technology, providing a solid foundation for his future endeavors.

Example: As a child, Ritchie often watched his father, Alistair Ritchie, work on complex electronic circuits in their basement. Fascinated by the intricate designs and functionality of these circuits, Ritchie developed a keen interest in understanding how machines work. This early exposure to technology eventually led him to pursue a career in computer science.

2. Academic pursuits and research

Ritchie's academic journey further shaped his work and introduced him to new ideas and concepts in computer science. His education at Harvard University and later at the Massachusetts Institute of Technology (MIT) provided him with a solid theoretical foundation, enabling him to apply his knowledge to real-world problems effectively.

Example: While studying at MIT, Ritchie had the opportunity to work on Project MAC (Multiple Access Computer), which laid the groundwork for his future contributions. This project exposed him to innovative programming languages and operating systems, fueling his interest in developing efficient and user-friendly software solutions.

3. Collaborative spirit and mentorship

Ritchie's experiences of working in collaborative environments and the mentorship he received played a crucial role in shaping his approach to programming. His collaboration with Ken Thompson, a fellow programmer, at Bell Labs had a profound impact on his work and the development of the C language.

Example: Working closely with Thompson, Ritchie was able to exchange ideas and explore new possibilities in programming. Their collaboration resulted in the creation of the Unix operating system and the development of the C language. The supportive and collaborative nature of their partnership fostered an environment of innovation and paved the way for future advancements in computer science.

4. Practical problem-solving approach

Ritchie's pragmatic and problem-solving mindset greatly influenced his work. He believed in developing practical solutions that could address real-world challenges faced by programmers and users alike. This approach made his work accessible and applicable in various domains.

Example: Ritchie's development of the C language and its associated tools, such as the C compiler, exemplified his practical problem-solving approach. By designing a concise and efficient programming language, he aimed to simplify the process of software development and improve the overall productivity of programmers. This approach revolutionized the field of programming and paved the way for future advancements in software engineering.

5. Experience-driven innovation

Ritchie's personal experiences and encounters with different technology-related challenges fueled his drive for innovation. He sought to address existing limitations and push the boundaries of what was possible in computer science. These experiences ultimately led to groundbreaking advancements and a lasting impact on the field.

Example: Ritchie's personal experiences with operating systems and programming languages highlighted the need for a simpler and more versatile language. His work on the development of the C language, inspired by the shortcomings of earlier languages, introduced a host of features that made programming more accessible and efficient. This experience-driven innovation laid the foundation for modern programming languages and influenced the evolution of software development practices.

In conclusion, Dennis Ritchie's personal experiences significantly influenced his work as a programmer. From early exposure to technology to collaborative partnerships and a practical problem-solving approach, his personal journey shaped his unique perspective on programming. By leveraging his experiences, Ritchie made groundbreaking contributions to computer science, leaving a lasting impact on the field and inspiring future generations of programmers.

Collaboration and teamwork

Ritchie's Partnership with Ken Thompson

The collaboration between Dennis Ritchie and Ken Thompson was nothing short of legendary. Their partnership laid the foundation for some of the most groundbreaking and influential innovations in computer science and programming. Ritchie's expertise in language design and Thompson's hardware and software engineering skills complemented each other perfectly, creating a synergy that propelled their work to new heights.

Their partnership began at Bell Labs in the late 1960s, where they were both part of a team working on the Multics operating system. However, they soon became disillusioned with the project and decided to branch out on their own. This decision marked the beginning of their remarkable journey together.

Together, Ritchie and Thompson embarked on the development of a new operating system called Unix. Ritchie's expertise in language design was instrumental in creating a powerful and flexible operating system that could be used on various hardware platforms. Thompson's expertise in hardware and software engineering ensured that Unix was not only efficient but also adaptable to different environments.

One of the key highlights of their partnership was the development of the C programming language. Ritchie's visionary ideas and Thompson's technical skills culminated in the creation of a language that would revolutionize programming. C became the lingua franca of programming languages, offering a balance between low-level control and high-level abstraction. It provided programmers with a powerful toolset to write efficient and portable code.

Their collaboration extended beyond the development of Unix and the C language. They worked together to build a culture of collaboration at Bell Labs, fostering an environment where ideas were freely shared and experimentation was encouraged. This collaborative spirit extended to other prominent programmers at Bell Labs, such as Brian Kernighan and Rob Pike, who also made significant contributions to the development of Unix and the C language.

Through their partnership, Ritchie and Thompson not only created groundbreaking technologies but also established a philosophy that would shape the future of computing. They believed in simplicity, elegance, and the power of abstraction. Their work on Unix and the C language laid the groundwork for the open-source movement, emphasizing the importance of sharing code and knowledge freely.

Their collaboration faced its fair share of challenges and obstacles. Limited resources and technology constraints tested their ingenuity. Competition from industry giants and criticism from skeptics motivated them to push the boundaries of what was possible. Through it all, their partnership thrived, and they persevered, leaving an indelible mark on the world of programming.

Ritchie and Thompson's partnership serves as a testament to the value of teamwork and collaboration in software development. It teaches us the importance of finding complementary skills and expertise in our colleagues and recognizing the power that can be unleashed when we work together towards a common goal.

In conclusion, the partnership between Dennis Ritchie and Ken Thompson was a force to be reckoned with. Their collaboration resulted in the creation of Unix, the C programming language, and a philosophy of simplicity and collaboration that continues to shape the world of programming. Their legacy serves as an inspiration to programmers, reminding us of the transformative power that can be achieved through a strong partnership and shared vision.

Building a culture of collaboration at Bell Labs

At Bell Labs, Dennis Ritchie played a pivotal role in building a culture of collaboration that fostered innovation and excellence. This culture was instrumental in the development of groundbreaking technologies such as the Unix operating system and the C language. In this section, we will explore the key elements that contributed to this culture and discuss the importance of collaboration in software development.

Creating an environment of trust and respect

An essential aspect of building a collaborative culture is creating an environment where trust and respect are paramount. Ritchie understood the importance of fostering strong relationships among team members, which allowed for open communication and the sharing of ideas. By treating everyone as equals and valuing their contributions, he established a sense of mutual respect that encouraged collaboration.

Example: One of the ways Ritchie promoted a collaborative environment was by organizing regular team meetings where team members could share their progress, challenges, and ideas. These meetings provided a platform for open discussions and constructive feedback, fostering a sense of trust and camaraderie within the team.

Encouraging interdisciplinary collaboration

Ritchie recognized that collaboration should not be limited to individuals within the same discipline or department. By encouraging interdisciplinary collaboration, he brought together experts from various fields, such as programming, mathematics, and engineering, to work towards common goals. This diverse range of perspectives enriched the development process and led to innovative solutions.

Example: In the development of the C language, Ritchie worked closely with Ken Thompson, who was an expert in operating systems. Their collaboration allowed them to combine their areas of expertise, resulting in the creation of a language that was not only powerful but also well-suited for building a new operating system like Unix.

Promoting knowledge sharing and mentorship

To foster collaboration, it is crucial to promote knowledge sharing and mentorship within the team. Ritchie understood that sharing knowledge and guiding others not only benefits the individuals involved but also enhances the collective expertise of the entire team. He actively encouraged senior members to mentor and guide junior team members, creating a culture of continuous learning and growth.

Example: Ritchie would often organize informal sessions where team members could share their knowledge and experiences. These sessions allowed individuals to learn from each other's expertise and also serve as a platform for mentoring. This collaborative learning environment accelerated the development of skills within the team and ensured the continuous improvement of their collective knowledge.

Emphasizing the importance of teamwork

Ritchie believed in the power of teamwork and its ability to accomplish great things. He understood that by working together towards a common goal, teams can achieve more than what any individual can accomplish alone. He fostered a culture where the success of the team was celebrated, and individual achievements were recognized as contributions to the collective effort.

Example: When the Unix operating system was developed, Ritchie ensured that recognition was given to the entire team for their contributions. This acknowledgment not only motivated team members but also reinforced the idea that collaboration and teamwork are essential for success.

Incorporating feedback and iteration

Collaboration is not just about working together; it also involves actively seeking and incorporating feedback from team members. Ritchie believed in the power of iterative development, where ideas are refined through continuous feedback loops. By creating a culture that valued feedback and iteration, he ensured that the resulting solutions were robust and built upon the collective wisdom of the team.

Example: In the development of the C language, Ritchie and his team constantly sought feedback from early users and industry experts. They used this feedback to improve the language, adding new features and refining its design. This iterative approach resulted in a language that was widely adopted and highly regarded for its elegance and efficiency.

The lasting impact of a collaborative culture

The collaborative culture established by Ritchie at Bell Labs has had a lasting impact on the software development industry. It has shown that teamwork, trust, and a commitment to shared goals can lead to groundbreaking innovations. The principles of collaboration pioneered by Ritchie continue to inspire and influence software developers to this day.

Caveat: While collaboration is essential, it is also important to strike a balance with individual autonomy and creativity. It is crucial to provide space for individuals to explore their ideas and contribute their unique perspectives. This balance between collaboration and individuality is what truly fuels innovation.

In conclusion, building a culture of collaboration at Bell Labs was key to the success and impact of Dennis Ritchie's work. By creating an environment of trust, encouraging interdisciplinary collaboration, promoting knowledge sharing and mentorship, emphasizing teamwork, and incorporating feedback and iteration,

Ritchie laid the foundation for innovation and excellence. The lessons learned from his collaborative approach continue to shape the way software development teams collaborate and create today.

Working with other prominent programmers

Working with other prominent programmers was a key aspect of Dennis Ritchie's career. Throughout his life, he had the opportunity to collaborate and learn from some of the brightest minds in the field. In this section, we will explore Ritchie's experiences working with other programmers, the lessons he learned, and the importance of collaboration in software development.

Building a network of talented individuals

Dennis Ritchie recognized the value of surrounding himself with talented individuals. He actively sought out opportunities to work with other programmers who shared his passion for innovation and problem-solving. One of the most notable collaborations in Ritchie's career was his partnership with Ken Thompson. Together, they laid the foundation for the development of the Unix operating system and the C programming language.

Ritchie's partnership with Thompson was a perfect example of complementary skills coming together. While Ritchie excelled in language design and low-level programming, Thompson brought his expertise in operating systems and hardware. This collaboration allowed them to combine their strengths and create groundbreaking technologies that heavily influenced the field of computer science.

Beyond his partnership with Thompson, Ritchie also worked with other prominent programmers at Bell Labs, where he spent the majority of his career. These collaborations fostered an environment of constant learning and knowledge exchange. Among his colleagues were Brian Kernighan, who co-authored "The C Programming Language" with Ritchie, and Jon Bentley, a renowned computer scientist and author.

Lessons learned from working in a team

Working with other talented programmers taught Ritchie valuable lessons that shaped his approach to software development. One important lesson was the power of collaboration and teamwork. Ritchie recognized that bringing together individuals with diverse perspectives and skills could lead to more innovative solutions.

In a team setting, different programmers bring their unique expertise and problem-solving approaches to the table. This diversity of thought enables more comprehensive analysis of problems and fosters creative thinking. Ritchie understood the importance of creating an environment that encouraged open communication and the free exchange of ideas.

Another crucial lesson learned from working with other prominent programmers was the importance of code review and constructive criticism. Collaborative programming involves reviewing each other's code to spot errors, suggest improvements, and ensure adherence to coding standards. Through this process, Ritchie and his collaborators refined their code, ensuring that it was robust and maintainable.

Moreover, Ritchie discovered the value of mentorship and learning from more experienced programmers. Working alongside experienced individuals allowed him to gain insights into best practices and established techniques. It also inspired him to continually improve his skills and expand his knowledge base.

The importance of collaboration in software development

Dennis Ritchie's experiences working with other prominent programmers emphasized the importance of collaboration in software development. Successful projects often require a team effort, with individuals bringing their expertise and unique insights to the table.

Collaboration enables programmers to take on larger and more complex projects that may not be feasible for a single individual. It facilitates knowledge sharing, prevents tunnel vision, and encourages creativity. By pooling their strengths, programmers can collectively overcome challenges and produce higher quality results.

Another benefit of collaboration is the opportunity for continuous learning and growth. By working with other talented programmers, individuals can broaden their skill sets, gain new perspectives, and expand their knowledge in different areas of programming.

Additionally, collaboration promotes accountability and shared responsibility. Team members can hold each other accountable for their work, ensuring that everyone is pulling their weight and contributing to the project's success. This fosters a sense of collective ownership and motivates individuals to perform at their best.

In today's software development industry, collaboration is further facilitated by modern technologies. Version control systems like Git allow programmers to work on the same codebase simultaneously, merging their changes seamlessly.

Communication tools such as Slack and project management platforms like Jira enable efficient collaboration, even with remote team members.

However, collaboration does come with challenges. It requires effective communication, mutual respect, and a willingness to compromise. Individuals must learn to navigate conflicting ideas and find common ground. Successful collaboration also relies on clear roles and responsibilities, with each team member understanding their contribution to the project.

Real-world example: Open-source projects

One compelling example of the power of collaboration is the development of open-source software projects. Open-source projects are typically developed by a community of contributors who work together to create and improve software. Dennis Ritchie himself was involved in the development of Unix, which is considered one of the earliest successful open-source projects.

Open-source projects allow programmers from all around the world to collaborate, regardless of their geographic location or institutional affiliations. Contributors can share their knowledge, expertise, and code, benefiting from the collective intelligence and effort of the community.

This collaborative model has given rise to widely used software such as the Linux operating system, the Apache web server, and the Python programming language. The success of these projects can be attributed to the vibrant communities behind them, with countless programmers coming together to contribute, review code, identify and fix bugs, and suggest improvements.

Open-source projects also provide an excellent platform for aspiring programmers to gain experience, learn from others, and showcase their skills. By contributing to open-source projects, individuals can demonstrate their ability to work collaboratively and make a tangible impact on widely used software.

Conclusion

Working with other prominent programmers played a crucial role in Dennis Ritchie's journey as a software developer. Through collaborations with individuals like Ken Thompson, Brian Kernighan, and Jon Bentley, Ritchie gained invaluable insights and experiences that shaped his approach to software development.

Ritchie's collaborations taught him the importance of collaboration and teamwork and highlighted the power of diverse perspectives and skills. He learned the value of constant learning, mentorship, and code review. These lessons influenced his work and contributed to the success of projects like Unix and the development of the C programming language.

Collaboration remains an essential aspect of software development today. It enables programmers to tackle complex problems, fosters creativity and innovation, and promotes continuous learning and growth. By working together, programmers can create groundbreaking technologies and shape the future of the field.

As the industry evolves, the principles of collaboration become even more critical. With the rise of remote work and distributed teams, effective communication and collaboration tools play a central role in facilitating productive teamwork. By embracing collaboration and learning from the experiences of pioneers like Dennis Ritchie, programmers can create a culture of innovation and build truly remarkable software.

Lessons learned from working in a team

Working in a team is a fundamental aspect of software development, and Dennis Ritchie's experience provides valuable lessons for programmers today. Ritchie's collaboration with Ken Thompson and his work at Bell Labs exemplify the power and importance of teamwork in achieving groundbreaking results. In this section, we will explore some key lessons learned from working in a team, drawing inspiration from Ritchie's experiences.

Lesson 1: Communication is key

One of the most crucial elements of successful teamwork is effective communication. It is essential to establish clear channels of communication and maintain open and transparent lines of dialogue. Ritchie greatly valued the power of communication, and his collaboration with Thompson and other programmers demonstrates the effectiveness of continuous and clear communication in achieving common goals.

Team members should actively listen to one another, share their ideas and concerns, and provide constructive feedback. Regular team meetings and project status updates are necessary to keep everyone informed, aligned, and motivated. By fostering a culture of open communication, team members can build trust, minimize misunderstandings, and maximize productivity.

Lesson 2: Embrace collaboration and diversity

Collaboration thrives on the diversity of perspectives, experiences, and skills that team members bring to the table. Ritchie's partnership with Ken Thompson exemplifies the power of collaboration between two individuals with complementary strengths. Their combined efforts resulted in the development of the C language and Unix, which revolutionized the software industry.

Teams should actively seek diversity and encourage every member to contribute their unique insights. By embracing different viewpoints and approaches, teams can discover innovative solutions and tackle complex challenges effectively. It is essential to foster an environment where every team member feels valued and empowered to make meaningful contributions.

Lesson 3: Establish clear roles and responsibilities

To ensure effective teamwork, it is crucial to establish clear roles and responsibilities for each team member. By defining individual responsibilities, team members can understand their specific contributions to the project and work towards achieving common goals. In the case of Ritchie's collaboration with Thompson, they had complementary roles and responsibilities, such as language design and implementation, respectively.

When assigning roles, project managers should take into account each team member's strengths, skills, and interests. Clear role definitions help avoid conflicts, improve accountability, and foster a sense of ownership among team members. Regularly reassessing and realigning roles and responsibilities based on evolving project needs is also essential.

Lesson 4: Foster a supportive and collaborative environment

A supportive and collaborative team environment is crucial for effective teamwork. Ritchie's work at Bell Labs is a testament to the importance of creating an environment that encourages knowledge sharing, idea exchange, and mutual support. The culture of collaboration at Bell Labs greatly contributed to the success of projects like the C language and Unix.

To foster a collaborative environment, team leaders should encourage respect, trust, and inclusivity. Team members should feel safe to express their opinions, ask questions, and seek help when needed. Celebrating achievements, recognizing individual contributions, and providing support in times of challenges or setbacks are vital in maintaining team morale and productivity.

Lesson 5: Learn from failures and embrace continuous improvement

Failure is an inevitable part of any team's journey. It is essential to view failures as opportunities for learning and growth. Ritchie's work was not without its challenges and setbacks, but he persevered and learned from those experiences. His ability to overcome obstacles and continuously improve his work contributed to his success.

Team members should approach failures with a growth mindset, seeking to understand the root causes and identifying areas for improvement. Regular project retrospectives and lessons learned sessions can help teams reflect on their experiences, celebrate successes, and identify strategies to overcome challenges in future projects. Continuous improvement should be a shared responsibility within the team.

In conclusion, Dennis Ritchie's experiences highlight the importance of teamwork in achieving remarkable results in software development. By emphasizing effective communication, embracing collaboration and diversity, establishing clear roles, fostering a supportive environment, and learning from failures, teams can maximize their potential and create groundbreaking solutions. Ritchie's example reminds us that the future of programming lies in collaborative efforts and collective intelligence.

The importance of collaboration in software development

Collaboration is a fundamental aspect of software development, and it plays a crucial role in the success of any project. It involves individuals working together, sharing knowledge, skills, and resources to achieve a common goal. In the context of software development, collaboration is not just about programmers writing code together, but also about effectively communicating and coordinating efforts across different teams and disciplines involved in the development process.

The significance of collaboration

Effective collaboration in software development brings numerous benefits that contribute to the overall success of a project. Here are some key reasons why collaboration is important:

1. **Improved problem-solving abilities:** Collaboration allows software developers to pool their collective knowledge and expertise, resulting in more innovative and creative solutions to complex problems. By working together, team members can identify potential issues, brainstorm ideas, and find effective solutions faster than if they were working alone.

2. **Enhanced efficiency and productivity:** When team members collaborate, tasks can be divided, allowing each individual to focus on their area of expertise. By leveraging their unique skills, team members can work more

efficiently, completing tasks faster and with higher quality. Collaboration also minimizes duplication of effort and avoids reinventing the wheel, leading to increased productivity.

3. **Increased software quality:** Collaboration enables continuous code review, knowledge sharing, and constructive feedback among team members. This iterative process helps identify and rectify errors, improve code readability, and enforce best practices. As a result, the software produced is of higher quality, with fewer bugs and better performance.

4. **Mitigation of risks and uncertainties:** Software development is inherently complex, with numerous risks and uncertainties. Collaboration allows team members to share their insights and experiences, helping to identify potential risks and devise strategies for risk mitigation. By leveraging the collective knowledge of the team, the project can navigate uncertain terrain more effectively.

5. **Stimulated innovation and creativity:** Collaboration fosters an environment that encourages the exchange of ideas, leading to increased innovation and creativity. By working together and challenging each other's perspectives, team members can come up with novel and out-of-the-box solutions. Additionally, diverse viewpoints and backgrounds contribute to the richness of ideas, enhancing the overall quality of the software.

Challenges and strategies for effective collaboration

While collaboration brings significant benefits to software development, it is not without its challenges. Here are some common challenges and strategies to address them:

1. **Communication barriers:** Effective communication is a cornerstone of collaboration. However, language barriers, different communication styles, and time zone differences can hinder effective collaboration. To address these challenges, teams can establish clear communication channels, leverage collaborative tools and technologies, and foster a culture of open and transparent communication. Regular meetings, both synchronous and asynchronous, can also help bridge communication gaps.

2. **Conflicting opinions and egos:** Collaboration can sometimes lead to conflicting opinions and clashes of egos, which can undermine the effectiveness of the team. To manage these conflicts, it is essential to foster a

culture of mutual respect, encourage open dialogue, and establish a process for constructive feedback and conflict resolution. Team members should focus on the shared goal and prioritize the best interest of the project over personal opinions.

3. **Coordination and task management:** In large software development projects, effective coordination and task management are crucial. Without proper coordination, team members might duplicate their efforts or miss critical dependencies. To address this challenge, teams can adopt project management methodologies such as Agile or Kanban, use collaborative task management tools, and establish clear roles and responsibilities. Regular progress updates and shared project documentation also help keep everyone informed.

4. **Cultural and diversity considerations:** Collaboration often involves individuals from diverse backgrounds and cultures. While diversity brings valuable perspectives, it can also lead to misunderstandings and communication gaps. It is essential to cultivate a culture of inclusivity, respecting and appreciating different viewpoints and experiences. Providing cultural sensitivity training and creating opportunities for team building activities can help foster empathy and understanding among team members.

5. **Knowledge sharing and documentation:** Collaboration is not just about teamwork but also about capturing and sharing knowledge. Without proper documentation and knowledge sharing mechanisms, team members might reinvent solutions or miss critical information. Establishing a shared knowledge repository, conducting regular code reviews, and documenting best practices and lessons learned help ensure knowledge is accessible and preserved.

Real-world example: Open-source collaboration

One of the most prominent examples of successful collaboration in software development is the open-source movement. Open-source projects rely on the collective efforts of a global community of developers who collaborate voluntarily to create and enhance software. This collaborative model has given rise to numerous widely-used software products, such as the Linux operating system and the Apache web server.

Open-source collaboration embodies the principles of transparency, inclusivity, and meritocracy. Developers from different backgrounds collaborate online, contributing code, reporting bugs, and suggesting improvements. Collaboration takes place through distributed version control systems like Git, public issue trackers, and community forums.

The success of open-source collaboration can be attributed to several factors. First, the distributed nature allows developers from around the world to contribute at their convenience, fostering a diverse and vibrant community. Second, the open nature of the development process and continuous peer review ensures high-quality code and minimizes the likelihood of errors. Third, the focus on meritocracy means that contributions are evaluated based on their technical value rather than the background or reputation of the contributor.

The open-source model also presents challenges, such as coordinating contributions from a large number of developers and managing competing priorities. However, the collaborative nature of open-source projects and the shared passion for creating high-quality software help overcome these challenges.

Conclusion

Collaboration is an essential ingredient for successful software development. It enables software developers to tap into their collective knowledge and expertise, resulting in improved problem-solving abilities, enhanced efficiency and productivity, increased software quality, reduced risks, and stimulated innovation. However, effective collaboration requires addressing challenges such as communication barriers, conflicting opinions, coordination issues, cultural considerations, and knowledge sharing.

By fostering a collaborative culture, leveraging collaborative tools and technologies, and embracing diversity, software development teams can reap the benefits of collaboration and create software that meets the needs of users, drives innovation, and advances the field of computer science. The open-source movement stands as a shining example of the power of collaboration in software development, showcasing the potential when individuals come together to create something greater than the sum of their parts.

Challenges and obstacles faced

Dealing with limited resources and technology constraints

In the early days of computer programming, Dennis Ritchie faced numerous challenges when dealing with limited resources and technology constraints. These obstacles influenced the development of the C language and shaped his approach to software design. In this section, we will explore some of the key challenges Ritchie encountered and the innovative solutions he devised.

The era of limited computing resources

During the 1960s and 1970s, computing resources were scarce and expensive. Computers were large, slow, and had limited memory and processing power. This posed significant constraints and limitations on the capabilities of programming languages and software systems.

Problem 1: Limited memory capacity   One major challenge Ritchie faced was the limited memory capacity of early computer systems. Programs had to fit within the available memory space, often resulting in trade-offs and compromises in functionality. This constraint led to the need for efficient memory management techniques to optimize program performance.

Solution: Memory-efficient programming   Ritchie recognized the importance of memory efficiency and designed the C language with features that allowed programmers to manage memory resources effectively. He introduced dynamic memory allocation through functions such as `malloc()` and `free()`, enabling programs to allocate and deallocate memory at runtime. This allowed for more flexible memory usage and efficient utilization of limited resources.

Problem 2: Limited processing power   Another significant constraint Ritchie faced was the limited processing power of early computers. Programs had to be designed to execute within the constraints of the available processing speed, which often required careful optimization.

Solution: Efficient code execution   To address the challenge of limited processing power, Ritchie focused on developing a language that prioritized efficiency and performance. The C language provided low-level programming capabilities, enabling programmers to write highly optimized code. Additionally, Ritchie incorporated features such as inline assembly code, which allowed developers to write machine-specific instructions for optimized execution.

Technology constraints and compatibility

In addition to limited computing resources, Ritchie also had to contend with technology constraints and compatibility issues. These challenges influenced the design of the C language and pushed for innovation in areas like portability and interoperability.

Problem 1: Diverse hardware architectures   During the early days of computer programming, there was a wide variety of hardware architectures in use. Each system had its own unique instruction set, data formats, and memory addressing modes. This posed a significant challenge for developers who needed to write code that could run on different machines.

Solution: Machine-independent programming   Ritchie recognized the need for a language that could be easily ported across different hardware architectures. He designed the C language to be machine-independent, allowing programmers to write code that could be compiled and executed on various systems without significant modifications. This portability made C a popular choice for writing system software that needed to work across different platforms.

Problem 2: Interoperability between languages   In the early days of software development, it was common for programs to be written in different programming languages. However, these languages often had limited interoperability, making it challenging to integrate code written in different languages.

Solution: Language interoperability   Ritchie recognized the importance of language interoperability and designed the C language with features that made it compatible with other programming languages. For example, C provides facilities for calling assembly code and linking with code written in other languages. This allowed developers to leverage existing code libraries and incorporate them into their C programs, promoting code reuse and facilitating collaboration between programmers using different languages.

Innovative approaches to resource optimization

To overcome resource constraints, Ritchie devised innovative approaches to resource optimization that pushed the boundaries of what was possible with limited technology. These strategies are still relevant today and continue to influence modern software development practices.

Problem 1: Efficient memory usage   Limited memory capacity necessitated efficient memory usage to maximize the performance of programs. Traditional programming languages often lacked the flexibility to manage memory effectively.

Solution: Pointers in C Ritchie introduced pointers as a fundamental feature of the C language. Pointers provided fine-grained control over memory access, allowing for efficient data structures and memory manipulation. This enabled programmers to optimize memory usage and build more efficient algorithms.

Problem 2: Overcoming hardware limitations Early computer systems had hardware limitations that posed challenges for software development, including limited support for input/output operations and multitasking.

Solution: **Leveraging low-level programming** Ritchie leveraged his understanding of low-level programming and system architecture to develop features in the C language that allowed programmers to interact directly with hardware. This included capabilities such as bit manipulation, direct memory access, and system-level control. By providing low-level access to hardware, programmers could overcome hardware limitations and unlock the full potential of the underlying system.

Problem 3: Efficiency without sacrificing readability A common challenge in programming is balancing efficiency with code readability. Highly optimized code often sacrifices readability, making it harder to understand and maintain.

Solution: Elegant code design Ritchie emphasized the importance of code readability and elegance. He believed that code should be easy to understand and maintain, even while striving for efficiency. By designing the C language with a compact syntax and providing a set of powerful yet intuitive programming constructs, Ritchie enabled programmers to write efficient code that remained readable and maintainable.

In summary, Dennis Ritchie's ability to innovate and find solutions to limited resources and technology constraints played a crucial role in the development of the C language. His focus on memory efficiency, code optimization, and portability laid the foundation for modern programming practices. Ritchie's approach continues to inspire programmers to overcome limitations, push boundaries, and create innovative solutions in the face of resource constraints.

Competing against industry giants

In the early days of the computer industry, Dennis Ritchie was faced with the daunting task of competing against industry giants. These giants included established companies such as IBM and DEC (Digital Equipment Corporation) that had a strong hold on the market and had already developed their own programming languages.

3.3.2.1 The challenge of market dominance

One of the biggest challenges Ritchie faced was breaking through the market dominance of existing programming languages. At the time, languages like Fortran and COBOL were widely used and had become the de facto standards in the industry. These languages were already supported by major hardware manufacturers and had a large user base.

Ritchie's development of the C language posed a direct challenge to these dominant players. C offered a more flexible and efficient programming language that could be used across different hardware platforms. However, convincing programmers and companies to adopt a new language required overcoming skepticism and resistance to change.

3.3.2.2 Leveraging the Unix operating system

One of the key strategies Ritchie employed to compete against industry giants was leveraging the Unix operating system. Unix provided an open and modular platform that allowed for easy integration of new software and hardware components.

By developing C as the primary programming language for Unix, Ritchie created a powerful combination that offered a compelling alternative to the existing systems. C's portability and efficiency, combined with the flexibility of Unix, made it an attractive choice for developers who wanted to break free from the limitations of proprietary systems.

3.3.2.3 Fostering a community of like-minded individuals

Another tactic that Ritchie used to compete against industry giants was fostering a community of like-minded individuals. He recognized the importance of collaboration and the power of collective knowledge in overcoming the challenges posed by established players.

Ritchie actively encouraged collaboration within the programming community, both within Bell Labs and beyond. He shared his ideas and innovations with others, and he welcomed feedback and contributions from fellow programmers. This collaborative mindset helped to build a network of supporters who shared his vision of open and accessible software.

3.3.2.4 Adapting to changing industry trends

Ritchie understood the importance of staying ahead of the curve and adapting to changing industry trends. As the computer industry evolved, new technologies, hardware platforms, and programming paradigms emerged. To remain competitive,

Ritchie continually updated and improved the C language to meet the evolving needs of developers.

By embracing emerging trends and incorporating them into the C language, Ritchie ensured that it remained relevant in a rapidly changing industry. This adaptability helped C maintain its position as one of the most widely used programming languages, even as newer languages entered the scene.

3.3.2.5 Lessons learned from competing against industry giants

The experience of competing against industry giants taught Ritchie invaluable lessons that remain relevant today:

- Embrace innovation: To compete with established players, it is crucial to embrace innovation and introduce new ideas that challenge the status quo. By offering something different, developers can attract attention and gain a foothold in the market.

- Build a strong community: Collaboration and community-building are essential for success. By fostering an environment of knowledge sharing and collaboration, developers can pool their resources, ideas, and expertise to overcome challenges and drive innovation.

- Adapt to change: The ability to adapt to changing industry trends and technological advancements is key to staying competitive. Developers must be willing to learn and evolve alongside the industry, incorporating new ideas and technologies into their work.

- Be persistent: Competing against industry giants requires perseverance. It is important to stay focused on the goal and not be deterred by setbacks or initial resistance. With determination and dedication, even the smallest players can make a significant impact.

In conclusion, Dennis Ritchie's journey of competing against industry giants was not an easy one, but through innovative ideas, collaboration, adaptability, and persistence, he was able to carve out a space for the C language in a market dominated by established players. His approach serves as an inspiration for aspiring programmers who face similar challenges in the modern tech industry.

Overcoming criticism and skepticism

In the world of programming, criticism and skepticism are inevitable. As an innovator and pioneer in the field, Dennis Ritchie faced his fair share of challenges and doubters. However, his determination and belief in the power of his work allowed him to overcome these obstacles and leave a lasting impact on the world of computer science.

One of the main criticisms Dennis Ritchie faced was the skepticism surrounding the C programming language itself. During a time when established programming languages like Fortran and COBOL dominated the industry, the introduction of a new language was met with skepticism. Critics argued that C was too simple and lacked the robustness necessary for complex programming tasks.

To address these concerns, Ritchie focused on showcasing the versatility and power of the C language through practical examples and real-world applications. He actively collaborated with other programmers and used their feedback to refine and improve the language further. By demonstrating the ability of C to handle both system-level programming and application development, Ritchie was able to silence many skeptics.

Another criticism Ritchie faced was the perceived lack of support and documentation for the C language. Some developers questioned whether C could compete with languages that already had extensive libraries and frameworks. However, Ritchie countered this criticism by actively engaging with the programming community and working on standardization efforts.

He made sure that documentation and reference materials for the C language were readily available, making it easier for developers to learn and adopt the language. Additionally, Ritchie's contributions to the development of the C compiler helped to simplify the process of writing and executing C code, further enhancing its accessibility.

Ritchie also emphasized the importance of practicality and efficiency in programming. Critics argued that the simplicity of C came at the cost of performance and efficiency. However, Ritchie believed that the power of the language lay in its ability to produce efficient and elegant code.

To address these concerns, Ritchie focused on optimizing the C compiler, making it capable of generating highly efficient machine code. He also encouraged developers to embrace the principles of structured programming and modular design to enhance code readability and maintainability.

To overcome skepticism and criticism, Ritchie relied on his strong belief in the importance of collaboration and open dialogue. He actively sought feedback from fellow programmers and incorporated their insights into the development of the C language. By continuously working to improve and refine his creation, Ritchie was able to establish the credibility and value of the C language.

In summary, Dennis Ritchie faced criticism and skepticism throughout his career, particularly regarding the C programming language. However, his determination, practical examples, and commitment to collaboration enabled him to overcome these challenges. Through his efforts, Ritchie solidified the significance of the C language and left a lasting impact on the world of computer science. His ability to address criticism and skepticism serves as a valuable lesson for programmers, emphasizing the importance of perseverance, practicality, and open-mindedness in the face of challenges.

Balancing innovation with practicality

Innovation and practicality have always been two important considerations in software development. Balancing these two aspects is crucial to creating successful and impactful products. In this section, we will explore how Dennis Ritchie, the brilliant mind behind the C language, was able to navigate the delicate balance between innovation and practicality in his work.

Understanding the need for innovation

In order to create groundbreaking solutions, it is essential to foster a culture of innovation. Ritchie understood that in order to push the boundaries of programming languages, he needed to think outside the box and challenge existing conventions. This mindset led to the development of the C language, which revolutionized the world of programming.

Ritchie's innovative approach can be seen in his creation of the C compiler. This tool allowed programs to be written in a high-level language and then translated into machine code, making programming more accessible and efficient. By introducing this compiler, Ritchie showcased his forward-thinking mindset and ability to solve complex problems in elegant ways.

Practicality as a guiding principle

While innovation is important, practicality is equally crucial in software development. Practical considerations ensure that the solutions are feasible, reliable, and can be easily adopted by others. Ritchie recognized the importance of practicality and made it a key principle in his work.

One of the ways Ritchie achieved practicality was through the design of the C language itself. He focused on simplicity and ease of use, making the language accessible to a wide range of programmers. By prioritizing practicality, Ritchie made the C language a powerful tool that could be effectively utilized by professionals and beginners alike.

Additionally, Ritchie's collaboration with Ken Thompson on the development of the Unix operating system demonstrated his practical approach to software development. They designed Unix to be modular and scalable, allowing it to be easily adapted to different hardware platforms. This practicality made Unix a widely adopted and influential operating system in both academic and commercial settings.

The art of balancing

Balancing innovation with practicality requires a delicate dance. Too much focus on innovation can result in complex and unwieldy solutions that are difficult to maintain and understand. On the other hand, an excessive emphasis on practicality may lead to stagnant and uninspiring products.

Ritchie tackled this challenge by constantly iterating and refining his ideas. He took the time to carefully consider the practical implications of his innovative solutions and made adjustments as needed. This iterative approach allowed him to strike a balance between pushing the boundaries of programming and creating tools that were practical and useful.

It is important for modern programmers to learn from Ritchie's example and strive for a similar balance. Embracing innovation while keeping practicality in mind can lead to the development of impactful and sustainable software solutions.

Real-world examples

To further illustrate the importance of balancing innovation with practicality, let's consider a couple of real-world examples:

- **Smartphone applications:** When creating a new application, developers must balance innovative features with practical considerations such as usability and performance. A groundbreaking feature may capture attention initially, but if the application is difficult to use or slows down the device, it will likely fail. Striking a balance between innovation and practicality ensures that the application meets users' needs effectively.

- **Self-driving cars:** Autonomous vehicle technology requires innovative algorithms and advanced sensors. However, practical considerations such as safety and regulatory compliance are of utmost importance. Balancing innovation with practicality in this context means developing cutting-edge technology while ensuring that the vehicles are reliable and can operate safely in real-world conditions.

By examining these real-world examples, we can see how the principles of balancing innovation with practicality apply beyond the realm of programming languages and software development.

Exercises

1. Identify a software product or application that you believe strikes a good balance between innovation and practicality. Explain your reasoning and provide examples to support your answer.

2. Think of a situation where innovation was prioritized at the expense of practicality. What were the consequences of this approach? How could practicality have been better incorporated into the solution?

3. Consider a project you have worked on or are currently working on. Reflect on the balance between innovation and practicality in that project. Are there any adjustments you could make to improve this balance? What lessons can you learn from Ritchie's approach?

Conclusion

Balancing innovation with practicality is a crucial aspect of software development. Dennis Ritchie's work on the C language and Unix serves as a testament to the power of finding this delicate balance. By combining innovative ideas with practical considerations, Ritchie was able to create long-lasting and impactful solutions. As programmers, we can learn from his example and strive to strike our own balance between pushing boundaries and delivering practical products that meet users' needs.

Lessons learned from overcoming challenges

When Dennis Ritchie embarked on his journey to create the revolutionary C language, he faced numerous challenges along the way. These obstacles tested his resilience and determination, but ultimately helped shape his character and his approach to software development. In this section, we will explore some of the lessons that Ritchie learned from overcoming these challenges and how they can inspire and guide future generations of programmers.

Lesson 1: Embrace limitations and innovate

One of the most significant challenges Ritchie faced was dealing with limited resources and technology constraints. During the early days of the C language, computer memory and processing power were scarce commodities. However, rather than being discouraged by these limitations, Ritchie embraced them as opportunities for innovation.

He developed a deep understanding of the underlying hardware and worked tirelessly to optimize his code for efficiency. This allowed programmers to write programs that were both powerful and compact, making the C language an ideal choice for resource-constrained environments. The lesson here is that limitations should not be seen as roadblocks, but rather as catalysts for creativity and innovation.

Lesson 2: Persistence is key

Ritchie faced stiff competition from industry giants who were already entrenched in the programming language market. Despite this, he persevered and continued to refine and improve the C language. He refused to be discouraged by criticism or skepticism, instead using it as motivation to prove the value of his work.

This lesson teaches us the importance of persistence in the face of challenges. In the fast-paced world of software development, setbacks are inevitable. However, by staying focused and determined, we can overcome obstacles and achieve our goals.

Lesson 3: Balance innovation with practicality

As a visionary programmer, Ritchie was constantly pushing the boundaries of what was possible. However, he also recognized the importance of practicality. He understood that a programming language must not only be powerful, but also easy to use and understand.

Ritchie's approach to balancing innovation with practicality is a valuable lesson for programmers today. While it's essential to stay current with the latest technologies and trends, we must also remember the importance of delivering practical solutions that solve real-world problems.

Lesson 4: Learn from criticism and collaboration

Ritchie welcomed criticism and valued collaboration. He understood that by opening himself up to feedback and working with others, he could refine his ideas and produce better results. Collaborating with Ken Thompson and other prominent programmers at Bell Labs allowed Ritchie to build a culture of collaboration that fostered innovation and breakthroughs.

This lesson teaches us the value of being open to criticism and the power of collaboration in software development. By engaging in constructive dialogue and seeking diverse perspectives, we can learn from each other's experiences and create better solutions.

Lesson 5: Adapt to change

In the ever-evolving world of technology, change is inevitable. Ritchie understood the importance of adapting to new developments and staying ahead of the curve. Despite the success of the C language, he continued to evolve and improve it to meet the changing needs of the software industry.

This lesson reminds us of the need to stay agile and embrace change. As programmers, we must constantly update our skills, learn new technologies, and adapt to the evolving demands of the industry.

Unconventional Example: The Iceberg Method

To illustrate the lesson of embracing limitations and innovating, let's consider the example of the "Iceberg Method" in project management. The Iceberg Method suggests that project managers should embrace constraints instead of fighting against them, similar to Ritchie's approach.

Just as an iceberg has only a small fraction visible above the water, a project may have limited resources, tight deadlines, or other constraints that are apparent. However, like the massive portion of an iceberg hidden beneath the water's surface, these constraints can serve as the fuel for creativity and innovation.

By accepting the limitations and focusing on the essence of the project, project managers can find innovative solutions that deliver the desired outcomes within the constraints. This approach encourages out-of-the-box thinking and can lead to breakthroughs in project delivery.

Conclusion

Dennis Ritchie's journey in creating the C language was not without its challenges. However, through perseverance, innovation, collaboration, and adaptability, he overcame these obstacles and left a lasting impact on the world of programming. The lessons he learned from these challenges continue to inspire and guide programmers today. By embracing limitations, persisting in the face of adversity, balancing innovation with practicality, learning from criticism and collaboration, and adapting to change, we can navigate the ever-evolving landscape of software development and make our mark on the industry.

Chapter Four: Impact and Influence

The impact of Ritchie's work on computer science

The C language in academia

In the world of academia, the C programming language holds a special place. Widely regarded as one of the most influential and foundational programming languages, C has shaped the way computer science is taught and practiced in universities and colleges worldwide. Let's explore the significance of the C language in academia, its pedagogical value, and the impact it has had on the education of future programmers.

The pedagogical value of C

One of the reasons why the C language is highly valued in academia is its simplicity and elegance. C provides a clean and concise syntax, making it easier for newcomers to understand fundamental programming concepts. Its structured approach to programming, with its emphasis on functions and modular design, allows students to grasp the core principles of programming in a systematic manner.

Moreover, C is a low-level language, allowing students to gain a deeper understanding of how computers work at the hardware level. By learning C, students become acquainted with concepts such as memory management, pointers, and bitwise operations, which are essential for efficient programming and optimizing code. This knowledge lays a strong foundation for more advanced topics in computer architecture and systems programming.

Teaching problem-solving skills with C

The C language is also highly valued for its ability to foster critical thinking and problem-solving skills in students. Programming in C requires students to think algorithmically and develop logical solutions to complex problems. The process of breaking down a problem into smaller, manageable steps, designing algorithms, and translating them into C code helps students cultivate analytical thinking, attention to detail, and the ability to decompose problems into logical components.

Furthermore, C encourages students to develop good programming practices, such as code organization, documentation, and testing. By adhering to these practices, students learn how to write clean, maintainable, and efficient code, which is crucial not only for academic projects but also for industry-level programming.

Applying C principles in other areas

Beyond its pedagogical value, the C language finds applications in various areas of academia. For instance, C is widely used in scientific research, especially in areas such as numerical computation, simulations, and data analysis. Its efficient memory management and low-level operations make it a preferred choice for researchers working with large datasets or computationally intensive algorithms.

Additionally, C is often employed in the development of embedded systems, where control over hardware and efficient resource allocation are paramount. Many academic courses and research projects in fields like robotics, automotive systems, and aerospace engineering heavily rely on C for their implementations.

Industry collaboration and internships

Academic institutions actively collaborate with industry partners to bridge the gap between theoretical knowledge and practical application. The prevalence of C in the industry makes it crucial for universities to introduce the language early in their curriculum. By doing so, students become well-equipped with the skills needed to secure internships or job placements in industries that rely heavily on C programming.

Furthermore, industry collaboration also brings real-world projects and case studies into the academic setting. Students have the opportunity to work on challenging projects that require the application of C programming principles and gain hands-on experience in solving industry-specific problems. This interaction between academia and industry helps students develop a comprehensive understanding of the C language's practical applications and prepares them for future careers in the software industry.

Challenges in teaching C

Teaching the C language comes with its own set of challenges. One common difficulty is the initial learning curve, as C's low-level nature and emphasis on manual memory management can be daunting for beginners. Instructors must carefully design curriculum and teaching materials that gradually introduce these concepts, ensuring students are provided with ample practice and support to build confidence in their abilities.

Another challenge is keeping pace with the evolving nature of the C language and its ecosystem. C is a mature language that has undergone numerous revisions and enhancements over the years. It is crucial for educators to stay up-to-date with the latest developments, striking a balance between teaching the core principles while incorporating modern features and best practices.

Conclusion

The C language has played a crucial role in academia, revolutionizing computer science education and shaping the minds of future programmers. Its simplicity, low-level nature, and emphasis on problem-solving make it an excellent language for teaching fundamental programming concepts. Additionally, C's applications in scientific research, embedded systems, and industry collaborations further solidify its significance in the academic realm.

As the landscape of computer science continues to evolve, it is important for academic institutions to adapt their curriculum to incorporate the latest advancements in the C language. By doing so, they ensure that students are well-prepared to take on the challenges of the modern programming world and continue building upon the enduring legacy of Dennis Ritchie.

The role of C in the development of operating systems

Operating systems serve as the backbone of modern computers, enabling them to efficiently run applications, manage system resources, and provide a user-friendly interface. The development of operating systems has evolved significantly over the years, with different programming languages playing a crucial role. In this section, we will explore the pivotal role that the C language has played in the development of operating systems.

Background and Principles of Operating Systems

To understand the significance of the C language in operating systems, it is essential to grasp the fundamental principles underlying these complex software systems. An operating system serves as an intermediary between hardware and software applications, providing a layer of abstraction for efficient resource management and process execution. It ensures that different programs can run concurrently, manages memory allocation, and facilitates communication between hardware and software components.

Historically, operating systems were primarily developed using low-level programming languages like assembly language. However, programming in assembly language was time-consuming, error-prone, and machine-specific, making it challenging to write portable and maintainable code. This led to the need for a high-level language that offered both flexibility and performance.

The Advent of the C Language

The birth of the C language, developed by Dennis Ritchie at Bell Labs in the early 1970s, brought about a paradigm shift in operating system development. C provided a higher level of abstraction than assembly language while still allowing for low-level system access. Its simplicity, portability, and efficiency made it an ideal choice for developing operating systems.

The C language offered features like structured programming, efficient memory management, and direct access to hardware resources. Its syntax closely resembled the mathematical notation and facilitated expressing complex ideas concisely. These characteristics made C an effective tool for implementing the intricate logic and algorithms required by operating systems.

Advantages of Using C in Operating Systems

1. **Portability:** C's design philosophy of being a low-level language with high-level features made it highly portable. Operating systems written in C could be easily ported across different hardware architectures and significantly reduced the development time for supporting new platforms.

2. **Efficiency:** C provided direct access to memory and hardware resources, allowing operating systems to be implemented with optimal performance. The language allowed fine-grained control over system resources and efficient manipulation of data structures, crucial for managing complex tasks like process scheduling and memory allocation.

3. **Compatibility:** C's backward compatibility with assembly language facilitated the integration of legacy code written in assembly into operating systems developed in C. This enabled the reuse of existing system code and made the transition to C-based operating systems smoother.

4. **Flexibility:** The flexibility of the C language allowed operating system developers to implement a wide range of functionalities and tailor the system to specific requirements. Additionally, C's rich set of libraries provided a wealth of utility functions for handling complex tasks, such as file system management and network programming.

5. **Interoperability:** C's unique ability to interface with assembly language and other programming languages made it possible to incorporate device drivers and system utilities written in different languages into C-based operating systems. This interoperability expanded the capabilities of operating systems and facilitated their integration with a variety of applications.

Real-World Examples

One prominent example of an operating system that heavily relies on the C language is UNIX. Developed by Ken Thompson and Dennis Ritchie themselves, UNIX was written entirely in C. The use of C allowed UNIX to be portable across different hardware platforms and played a significant role in its widespread adoption.

Another example is the Linux operating system, which is modeled after UNIX and bears the influence of C. Linux's kernel, the heart of the operating system, is primarily implemented in C. The simplicity and efficiency of C continue to be instrumental in facilitating the development and maintenance of the Linux kernel.

Caveats and Challenges

While the C language has been instrumental in the development of operating systems, it is not without its challenges. The low-level nature of C makes it prone to certain types of programming errors, such as buffer overflow and memory leaks. These vulnerabilities can lead to system crashes or security breaches, necessitating robust testing and rigorous code reviews.

Furthermore, as operating systems become more complex and require increased performance, alternative programming languages like Rust are gaining popularity. Rust aims to provide memory safety guarantees while maintaining performance, addressing some of the challenges associated with C-based operating systems.

Conclusion

The C language has played a pivotal role in the development of operating systems, providing efficiency, portability, and flexibility. From its inception in Bell Labs to its impact on seminal operating systems like UNIX and Linux, C has revolutionized the way operating systems are developed and continues to shape the field.

As the software ecosystem evolves, new challenges and opportunities arise. While alternative languages may address some of the shortcomings of C, the longevity and continued relevance of the C language in operating systems cannot be underestimated. It remains an essential skill for understanding the foundations of operating system design and for carrying forward Dennis Ritchie's legacy of innovation and collaboration in programming.

C as a foundation for software development

The C programming language, created by Dennis Ritchie, has stood the test of time and continues to be a crucial foundation for software development. Its simplicity, efficiency, and versatility make it an essential tool for programmers working on a wide range of applications.

Simplicity and Efficiency

One of the key reasons for the success of the C language as a foundation for software development is its simplicity. The syntax of C is straightforward and easy to understand, making it accessible to programmers of all levels. It provides a concise and intuitive way to express complex ideas, allowing developers to write efficient and readable code.

The efficiency of C stems from its low-level nature. It provides direct control over the computer's hardware, allowing programmers to optimize their code for maximum performance. By utilizing features such as pointers and bitwise operations, C enables developers to write code that executes quickly and uses system resources efficiently.

Portability and Compatibility

C's compatibility with different hardware platforms and operating systems is another factor that has made it a foundation for software development. The language was designed to be easily portable, allowing programs written in C to run on different systems with minimal modifications. This flexibility has been crucial in the development of cross-platform applications and software libraries.

Furthermore, C has played a pivotal role in the creation of higher-level programming languages. Many popular programming languages, such as C++, Java, and Python, have been influenced by C and share similar syntax and concepts. This compatibility allows developers to seamlessly integrate code written in different languages, making C an essential part of modern software development.

Memory Management and Control

Another significant aspect of C as a foundation for software development is its memory management capabilities. C provides direct control over memory allocation and deallocation, giving programmers the freedom to manage system resources efficiently. This control is essential in scenarios where memory usage must be optimized or when real-time performance is critical.

However, with great power comes great responsibility. The manual memory management feature of C can be challenging for inexperienced programmers, as it requires careful attention to detail to avoid memory leaks and other memory-related issues. It is crucial for developers to have a solid understanding of memory management concepts, such as pointers, dynamic memory allocation, and deallocation, to write robust and error-free code.

Real-World Examples

To illustrate the importance of C as a foundation for software development, let's consider a real-world example. Imagine you are tasked with developing a device driver for a new graphics card. The driver needs to communicate directly with the hardware, perform efficient memory management, and have low-level access to device registers. These requirements perfectly align with the strengths of C, making it the ideal language for this task.

In this scenario, the simplicity, efficiency, and low-level control provided by C allow developers to write highly optimized code that seamlessly interacts with the hardware. The ability to directly manipulate memory and access device registers leads to faster and more efficient device driver performance, ultimately improving the overall user experience.

Resources and Caveats

While C offers many advantages as a foundation for software development, it also comes with certain challenges and caveats. Its low-level nature requires developers to have a good understanding of computer architecture and memory management concepts. In addition, C's flexibility can lead to potential pitfalls, such as buffer overflows and undefined behavior, if not carefully managed.

To mitigate these challenges, developers should take advantage of the vast resources available, including books, online tutorials, and community forums. These resources provide valuable insights, best practices, and techniques for writing robust and error-free C code. By continuously updating their knowledge and staying engaged with the C programming community, developers can harness the full potential of C as a foundation for software development.

Conclusion

In conclusion, the C programming language serves as a powerful foundation for software development. Its simplicity, efficiency, and versatility make it an essential tool for programmers across various domains. Whether developing device drivers, operating systems, or high-performance applications, C provides the necessary control and flexibility required to tackle complex programming tasks. By understanding and leveraging the strengths of C, developers can create robust, efficient, and portable software solutions that truly stand the test of time.

The longevity of the C language

The C language, created by Dennis Ritchie, has stood the test of time and continues to be one of the most enduring programming languages in existence. Its longevity can be attributed to several key factors that have ensured its relevance and widespread usage over the decades.

Efficiency and Performance

One of the primary reasons for the longevity of the C language is its efficiency and performance. C is a low-level language that provides direct access to the machine's hardware, allowing programmers to write code that executes quickly and utilizes system resources efficiently. This level of control over the hardware is essential in domains where performance is critical, such as system programming, embedded systems, and real-time applications.

For example, consider the automotive industry, where the C language has been extensively used for programming the engine control units (ECUs) in vehicles. These ECUs require precise timing and fast execution to control various components, including fuel injection, ignition, and emissions. The efficiency and performance offered by the C language make it an ideal choice for such applications.

Portability

Another crucial factor contributing to the longevity of the C language is its portability. C code can be easily compiled and executed on different platforms, including various operating systems and hardware architectures. This portability is achieved through the use of standardized libraries and the adherence to a set of well-defined language rules.

The portability of C has been instrumental in its widespread adoption and its use in developing cross-platform applications and systems. For instance, large-scale software projects like the GNU Compiler Collection (GCC) and the Linux operating system have been developed using C, enabling them to run on a wide range of platforms.

Interoperability

C's interoperability with other programming languages has also contributed to its longevity. C supports the concept of function prototypes, allowing programmers to interface with code written in other languages like C++, Python, and Java. This feature enables code reuse, as different modules of a project can be written in different languages while still being able to communicate with each other through C interfaces.

For instance, the Python programming language relies heavily on C interfaces to access low-level system libraries and optimize performance-critical modules. The ability to seamlessly integrate C code with Python has made it a popular choice among developers working on scientific computing, machine learning, and web development.

Stability and Standardization

The stability and standardization of the C language have played a significant role in its longevity. The C programming language has been standardized by international organizations like the International Organization for Standardization (ISO) and the American National Standards Institute (ANSI). These standards define the syntax, semantics, and behavior of C, ensuring consistency across various implementations.

The stability of the language means that code written in C decades ago can still be compiled and run on modern systems without significant modifications. This backward compatibility allows legacy systems and software written in C to continue functioning without the need for rewriting or upgrading.

Community and Ecosystem

The vibrant community and ecosystem surrounding the C language have also contributed to its longevity. C has a large and active user community that continues to create libraries, frameworks, and tools, enhancing the language's capabilities and solving new challenges.

One prominent example of this is the C Standard Library, which provides a rich set of functions for common tasks like input/output operations, string manipulation, and memory management. Additionally, there are numerous third-party libraries and frameworks, such as the OpenSSL cryptographic library and the GTK GUI toolkit, that have further expanded the capabilities of C.

The availability of extensive documentation, tutorials, and community forums ensures that new programmers can easily learn C and receive assistance when faced with challenges. This support system keeps the language relevant and accessible to both novice and experienced programmers.

Example: The Internet and C

To highlight the longevity of the C language, let's consider its role in the development of the internet. The internet, as we know it today, relies heavily on low-level network protocols like TCP/IP, which were implemented using the C language.

The creation of the C language and its subsequent adoption allowed developers to build the fundamental infrastructure of the internet, enabling communication and data transfer across networks. Even with the emergence of higher-level languages and web development frameworks, the foundational components of the internet continue to be built and maintained using C.

Further Reading and Resources

To delve deeper into the longevity of the C language and its impact on computer science, here are some recommended resources:

- "The C Programming Language" by Brian W. Kernighan and Dennis M. Ritchie - This book, often referred to as "K&R", is the definitive guide to C and provides insights into the language's design and principles.

- "C: A Reference Manual" by Samuel P. Harbison and Guy L. Steele Jr. - This comprehensive reference manual covers the C language standards and serves as a valuable resource for both beginners and experienced programmers.

- "C Interfaces and Implementations: Techniques for Creating Reusable Software" by David R. Hanson - This book explores the concept of interfaces in C and demonstrates how to create reusable and modular code, an essential aspect of modern software development.

- "Programming in C" by Stephen G. Kochan - This beginner-friendly book provides a hands-on introduction to programming in C and covers essential concepts, syntax, and best practices.

- The C Programming Language Specification - The official specification of the C language, available online, provides an in-depth understanding of the language and its features.

By understanding the efficiency, portability, interoperability, stability, and community surrounding the C language, we can appreciate its longevity and ongoing relevance in the ever-evolving field of computer science.

Note: The examples and illustrations in this subsection are intended to provide context and understanding of the topic at hand. They may not cover all aspects and considerations related to the longevity of the C language. They are not exhaustive proofs or formal explanations, but rather, practical and relatable scenarios aimed at engaging the reader.

The ongoing relevance of Ritchie's ideas and concepts

Dennis Ritchie's ideas and concepts continue to have a profound impact on the field of computer science and programming. His work, particularly the development of the C language, laid the foundation for modern software development and remains relevant to this day. In this section, we will explore the ongoing relevance of Ritchie's ideas and concepts, discussing their importance and influence in the rapidly evolving world of programming.

The versatility of the C language

One of the key reasons for the ongoing relevance of Ritchie's ideas and concepts is the versatility of the C language. C is a powerful and flexible programming language that allows programmers to write efficient and high-performance code across various domains and platforms. Its simplicity and low-level nature provide programmers with fine-grained control over hardware, making it ideal for systems programming, embedded systems, and operating system development.

The C language's versatility is evident in its widespread adoption in different industries and applications. From the development of operating systems like UNIX and Linux to the creation of embedded systems and microcontrollers, C has proven itself to be a reliable and efficient choice. Even in modern web development, where high-level languages like JavaScript and Python dominate, C remains essential for building foundational software components and optimizing performance-critical sections of code.

The influence of the C language on other programming languages

Ritchie's ideas and concepts, as embodied in the C language, have greatly influenced the development of subsequent programming languages. Many popular languages, such as C++, Java, and C#, have their roots in C and have built upon its foundations to provide higher-level abstractions and additional features.

For example, C++ introduced object-oriented programming (OOP) features to C, allowing programmers to organize code in a modular and reusable manner. Java, influenced by C and C++, introduced automatic memory management through garbage collection, making it easier to write robust and secure software. C#, another language heavily inspired by C and C++, combines the power of these languages with features tailored for Windows development.

The influence of the C language on other programming languages underscores its ongoing relevance and the lasting impact of Ritchie's ideas and concepts on the wider programming community.

The portability and adaptability of C-based systems

Another aspect of Ritchie's work that remains relevant today is the portability and adaptability of C-based systems. The development of the C language and its implementation on different platforms enabled software to be written once and run on multiple systems.

The concept of "write once, run anywhere" is a fundamental principle of modern software development. It allows developers to create software that can be deployed on various operating systems and hardware architectures without significant modifications. This portability greatly reduces development time and effort while increasing the reach and impact of software.

The portability and adaptability of C-based systems have also contributed to the success of open-source software. Many open-source projects, such as the Linux operating system, are written in C or C++ due to the portability and performance benefits these languages offer. This, in turn, has fostered collaboration and innovation within the programming community, as developers from different backgrounds can contribute to and benefit from shared codebases.

Efficiency and optimization

Ritchie's emphasis on efficiency and optimization in software development continues to be of utmost importance in today's computing landscape. As hardware capabilities have advanced, software has become increasingly complex and resource-intensive. Therefore, the ability to write efficient code that maximizes performance and minimizes resource usage is crucial.

The C language's low-level nature and direct access to hardware allow programmers to fine-tune their code for optimal performance. By leveraging low-level constructs such as pointers and bit manipulation, C programmers can write code that meets strict performance requirements, making it indispensable in fields such as game development, embedded systems, and real-time applications.

Furthermore, the principles of efficiency and optimization that Ritchie championed extend beyond the C language itself. They inform best practices in programming, influencing the design and implementation of high-level languages and frameworks. Developers today, regardless of the language they use, are mindful of performance considerations and strive to write code that maximizes efficiency.

The ongoing evolution of the C language

Lastly, the ongoing evolution of the C language itself showcases the relevance of Ritchie's ideas and concepts. Despite being decades old, the C language continues to evolve and adapt to meet the changing needs of the programming community.

Standardization efforts, such as the ISO/IEC C standards, ensure that the language remains relevant and compatible across different implementations. New features and enhancements are introduced in subsequent versions of the C language, addressing modern programming paradigms and improving developer productivity.

The ongoing evolution of the C language is a testament to its enduring value and the commitment of the programming community to carry forward Ritchie's legacy. It also reflects the adaptability and resilience of Ritchie's ideas and concepts, as they continue to shape the future of programming.

In conclusion, Ritchie's ideas and concepts, as embodied in the C language, remain relevant and influential in the field of computer science and programming. The versatility of C, its influence on other languages, and its portability and adaptability are testaments to its ongoing importance. Furthermore, Ritchie's emphasis on efficiency and optimization, as well as the ongoing evolution of the C language, ensure that his legacy continues to thrive in an ever-changing technological landscape. By understanding and appreciating Ritchie's ideas and concepts, programmers can draw inspiration and guidance to drive innovation and collaboration in the future of programming.

Inspiring future generations of programmers

The influence of Ritchie on young programmers

Dennis Ritchie's work and contributions have had a profound influence on young programmers around the world. His revolutionary creation, the C language, has become a fundamental building block for teaching and learning programming. In this section, we will explore the ways in which Ritchie's work continues to shape and inspire the new generation of programmers.

The enduring popularity of C

One of the main reasons why Ritchie's influence on young programmers is so significant is the enduring popularity of the C language. Despite being over 40 years old, C remains one of the most widely used programming languages today. It is the language of choice for systems programming, embedded systems, and low-level programming.

Many young programmers are attracted to C because of its simplicity, elegance, and efficiency. It provides a level of control and flexibility that is unmatched by higher-level languages. For aspiring programmers who want to understand how computers work at a lower level, learning C is often the first step. This trend can be attributed directly to Ritchie's vision and design of the language.

Learning the fundamentals

Ritchie's influence on young programmers goes beyond the popularity of the C language itself. His emphasis on fundamental programming concepts and principles has been instrumental in shaping programming education. The C language is often used as a teaching tool to help students grasp the core concepts of programming.

By learning C, young programmers gain a solid foundation in algorithm development, memory management, and control flow. They learn to work with variables, data types, and pointers, which are essential skills in any programming language. The emphasis on efficiency and resource management in C also instills good programming habits and an appreciation for optimization.

Understanding the roots of modern programming

Another way Ritchie influences young programmers is by fostering an understanding of the roots of modern programming. By studying C, aspiring programmers gain insight into the historical context and evolution of programming languages. They learn about the techniques and concepts that paved the way for the high-level languages and frameworks they use today.

In addition, understanding the C language helps young programmers appreciate the underlying mechanics of modern programming languages. They can better understand the trade-offs involved in language design and implementation. This knowledge gives them a broader perspective on programming and enables them to make informed decisions when choosing tools and technologies.

Applying Ritchie's principles in modern programming

Ritchie's influence extends beyond the C language itself. His principles of simplicity, elegance, and efficiency continue to resonate with young programmers in their pursuit of effective and elegant solutions. They strive to write clean, readable code that solves problems efficiently and effectively.

Furthermore, Ritchie's collaborative and open-source approach to software development inspires young programmers to contribute to open-source projects and engage in online programming communities. They recognize the value of working together and sharing knowledge, just as Ritchie did during his collaboration with Ken Thompson and in the development of the Unix operating system.

Ritchie as a role model

Lastly, young programmers look up to Dennis Ritchie as a role model. His brilliance, humility, and dedication to his craft serve as inspiration. Ritchie's impact on the world of programming motivates young programmers to aim high, to push boundaries, and to seek innovative solutions to challenging problems.

By studying Ritchie's work and the principles he embodied, young programmers learn not only about programming but also about professionalism, collaboration, and the importance of leaving a lasting legacy. They understand that their contributions can make a difference and that they, too, can shape the future of programming.

Conclusion

Dennis Ritchie's influence on young programmers is far-reaching and multi-faceted. Through the popularity of the C language, the emphasis on foundational programming concepts, the understanding of programming history, the application of his principles, and the role modeling effect, Ritchie continues to shape the new generation of programmers.

As we move forward in the ever-evolving field of programming, it is crucial to acknowledge and appreciate the legacy left behind by pioneers like Dennis Ritchie. By embracing his ideas and building upon his work, young programmers can continue to push the boundaries of what is possible and make their own mark on the world of programming.

Education and training in the C language

Education and training in the C language plays a crucial role in preparing programmers for a successful career in computer science. Aspiring programmers need to develop a strong foundation in C as it forms the basis for many other programming languages and provides essential concepts and practices for software development. In this section, we will explore the importance of education and training in the C language, discuss effective learning strategies, and provide resources for gaining proficiency in C.

Understanding the basics

Before embarking on the journey of learning C, it is essential to understand its fundamental concepts. The C language is known for its simplicity and efficiency, which makes it a popular choice for system programming and embedded systems. To grasp the basics, learners should focus on the following key areas:

- **Syntax and structure:** Understanding the syntax and structure of C is crucial, as it forms the building blocks for writing correct and readable code. It includes concepts such as variables, data types, operators, control structures, and function declarations.

- **Memory management:** C requires manual memory management, which means programmers need to allocate and deallocate memory resources explicitly. Understanding concepts like pointers, memory allocation, and deallocation is essential for efficient memory usage.

+ **Input and output:** Learning how to interact with the user and external devices through input and output operations is a fundamental aspect of programming. Familiarity with C's input/output library functions enables programmers to read and write data from files, handle user input, and interface with hardware.

Effective learning strategies

Learning the C language can be an exciting yet challenging task. Here are some effective strategies to enhance the learning experience and build a strong foundation in C:

+ **Hands-on practice:** Practice is key to mastering any programming language, and C is no exception. Solve coding exercises and work on small projects to gain familiarity with the language's features and syntax. The more you write code, the better you will understand and retain the concepts.

+ **Read and analyze code:** Reading and analyzing existing code written in C can provide valuable insights into good programming practices and efficient problem-solving techniques. Explore open-source projects or textbooks with well-explained code examples to enhance your understanding.

+ **Engage in discussions and forums:** Participating in discussions and online forums dedicated to C programming can expand your knowledge and expose you to different perspectives. Share your ideas, ask questions, and learn from experienced programmers in the community.

+ **Pair programming:** Pair programming, where two programmers collaborate on solving problems, can significantly accelerate the learning process. Working with a partner allows you to learn from their expertise, exchange ideas, and spot errors more effectively.

+ **Experiment with projects:** Applying your knowledge to real-world projects helps solidify your understanding and gives you practical experience. Start with small projects such as building a calculator or a simple game, and gradually tackle more complex endeavors to challenge yourself.

Resources for learning C

To support your education and training in the C language, a wide range of resources are available:

+ **Books:** Books such as "The C Programming Language" by Brian Kernighan and Dennis Ritchie, the creators of C, provide a comprehensive introduction to the language. Other recommended books include "C Programming Absolute Beginner's Guide" by Greg Perry and Dean Miller, and "C Programming for the Absolute Beginner" by Michael Vine.

+ **Online tutorials and courses:** Several online platforms offer interactive tutorials and courses for learning C. Websites like Codecademy, Coursera, and Udemy provide structured lessons, exercises, and quizzes to improve your skills.

+ **Programming challenges and sites:** Platforms like LeetCode, HackerRank, and Project Euler provide a collection of programming challenges that allow you to practice your C coding skills. These challenges cover a wide range of difficulty levels and problem domains.

+ **Online communities and forums:** Online communities such as Stack Overflow, Reddit's r/C_Programming, and Cprogramming.com offer forums where programmers can seek help, share knowledge, and discuss C-related topics.

+ **Code Editors and IDEs:** Code editors and Integrated Development Environments (IDEs) like Visual Studio Code, Eclipse, and Code::Blocks provide features like syntax highlighting, auto-completion, and debugging capabilities that facilitate the writing and testing of C code.

Embracing the spirit of innovation

Learning and mastering the C language is not just about memorizing syntax and rules. It is about embracing the spirit of innovation and creativity that drove Dennis Ritchie and his contemporaries. As you progress in your C programming journey, remember to:

+ **Think critically:** Cultivate a mindset of critical thinking and problem-solving. Analyze problems from different angles and explore multiple approaches to find the most efficient and elegant solutions.

+ **Be curious and explorative:** Experimentation is the key to unlocking new possibilities. Don't hesitate to explore unconventional ideas and push the boundaries of what you can do with C.

+ **Contribute to the community:** Share your knowledge and contribute to the C programming community. Contribute to open-source projects, write tutorials or articles, and help others in their programming journey.

+ **Stay updated:** Computer science is a rapidly evolving field, and it is essential to stay updated with the latest developments in C and programming. Follow reputable websites, blogs, and conferences to stay current with new features, best practices, and emerging trends.

By embracing these principles, you can not only gain expertise in the C language but also become a creative and innovative programmer.

Conclusion

Education and training in the C language form the building blocks for a successful career in computer science and software development. By understanding the basics, employing effective learning strategies, utilizing available resources, and embracing the spirit of innovation, programmers can gain proficiency in C and lay the foundation for their future endeavors. As Dennis Ritchie's work continues to influence generations of programmers, it is essential to approach education and training in the C language with enthusiasm, determination, and a commitment to excellence. Remember, the journey of mastering C is not just about acquiring a skill; it is about joining a community of thinkers and creators, where the possibilities are endless.

The importance of understanding programming history

In order to truly appreciate the present and shape the future of programming, it is crucial to have a deep understanding of its history. Programming history not only encompasses the evolution of programming languages and techniques, but also the stories and experiences of the pioneers who shaped the field. By exploring programming history, we gain valuable insights into the challenges faced by early programmers and the solutions they devised, paving the way for modern computing.

1. **Learning from the past:** By understanding programming history, programmers can learn from the successes and failures of those who came before

them. It provides a wealth of knowledge, enabling them to avoid common pitfalls and make informed decisions in their own code. For example, studying the historical roots of memory management techniques can help programmers write more efficient and secure code, as they gain insights from previous challenges and solutions.

2. **Contextualizing current technologies**: As technology continues to advance at an astounding pace, it is essential to have a contextual understanding of current programming languages, frameworks, and tools. Knowing the historical origins of these technologies helps programmers to comprehend their underlying design principles, motivations, and trade-offs. For instance, understanding the history of object-oriented programming (OOP) can shed light on the reasons behind certain design patterns and coding conventions prevalent in modern OOP languages like Java and C++.

3. **Inspiration for innovation**: Programming history is rich with examples of groundbreaking innovations that have propelled the field forward. By studying these breakthroughs, programmers can find inspiration for their own creative solutions to complex problems. For instance, examining the development of the Smalltalk programming language and graphical user interfaces can spark new ideas for designing intuitive and user-friendly software.

4. **Preserving the legacy**: Programming history is not just about technologies, but also about the brilliant minds behind them. Understanding the contributions of programming pioneers fosters a sense of respect and appreciation for their work. It is important to preserve and share their stories to inspire future generations of programmers. By understanding programming history, we can keep the legacies of pioneers like Dennis Ritchie alive, ensuring that their contributions continue to influence and shape the field.

5. **Avoiding reinvention of the wheel**: Programming history offers a treasure trove of reusable solutions and best practices. By studying historical programming techniques, programmers can save time and effort by building upon existing knowledge and methods. For example, learning about the algorithms and data structures used in early programming can guide the development of more efficient and optimized solutions, rather than reinventing the wheel.

6. **Understanding the sociocultural context**: Programming history reveals how technology has interacted with and influenced societal changes. It provides insights into the challenges faced by marginalized groups in the field, such as women and people of color, and how their contributions have often been overlooked or undervalued. By understanding the sociocultural context of programming history, we can work towards a more inclusive and diverse industry, where everyone's contributions are acknowledged and celebrated.

To delve into programming history, programmers can explore various resources such as books, documentaries, online archives, and interviews with pioneers. It is important to approach programming history with curiosity and a thirst for knowledge. By understanding the origins and evolution of programming, we can build upon the foundations laid by the programming giants of the past and shape a brighter future for the field. So, let us embark on this journey through time and uncover the fascinating stories and lessons that programming history holds for us.

Cultivating curiosity and creativity in programming

Programming is not just about writing code; it is about thinking creatively and approaching problems with curiosity. In this section, we will explore how we can cultivate these essential qualities in programming and harness them to become better programmers.

The power of curiosity in programming

Curiosity is the driving force behind innovation and the fuel that propels us to explore new ideas and possibilities. In programming, curiosity allows us to ask "what if" questions and challenge the status quo. It encourages us to dig deeper, understand the underlying principles, and explore alternative solutions. Curiosity enables us to see beyond the obvious and discover new ways of solving problems.

To cultivate curiosity in programming, it is important to embrace a growth mindset. A growth mindset recognizes that intelligence and abilities can be developed through dedication and hard work. Instead of viewing mistakes as failures, a growth mindset sees them as opportunities for learning and improvement. When faced with a programming challenge, approach it with a sense of wonder and curiosity. Ask questions, experiment, and explore different possibilities. Nurture your curiosity by continuously seeking new knowledge and staying open to learning from others.

Embracing creativity in problem-solving

Creativity is the ability to think outside the box and come up with innovative solutions. It is the key to finding elegant and efficient ways of solving problems. In programming, creativity allows us to approach challenges from different angles and discover unconventional solutions. It enables us to combine existing ideas and technologies in new and exciting ways.

To cultivate creativity in programming, it is important to foster a creative environment. Surround yourself with diverse perspectives and ideas. Engage in brainstorming sessions with peers or participate in coding competitions. Experiment with different programming languages, frameworks, and tools. Take breaks and engage in activities that inspire you, such as reading, listening to music, or practicing mindfulness. Sometimes, stepping away from a problem can spark new ideas and fresh approaches.

Another way to enhance creativity in programming is to embrace the concept of playfulness. Treat programming as a creative endeavor and allow yourself the freedom to explore and make mistakes. Embrace the joy of creating something new and unique. Often, the most innovative solutions emerge from a playful mindset.

The role of "cross-training" in programming

In sports, cross-training refers to the practice of engaging in different exercises and activities to improve overall fitness and prevent burnout. In programming, a similar approach can be applied to cultivate curiosity and creativity. Engaging in activities outside of programming can broaden your perspective and inspire new ideas.

Consider exploring other domains such as art, music, or literature. These disciplines can provide fresh insights and fuel your creativity. For example, studying graphic design can enhance your understanding of user interfaces and aesthetics in programming. Learning a musical instrument can sharpen your sense of rhythm and problem-solving skills.

Additionally, challenging yourself to solve real-world problems can stimulate creativity. Volunteer for open-source projects or collaborate with individuals from different backgrounds. Engaging with real-world problems exposes you to diverse perspectives and forces you to think creatively to find viable solutions.

Practical tips for cultivating curiosity and creativity

Here are some practical tips to foster curiosity and creativity in your programming journey:

+ Always ask "why" and seek to understand the underlying principles.

+ Read widely in diverse domains to broaden your knowledge and perspective.

+ Participate in coding competitions and challenges to push your boundaries.

+ Collaborate with peers and learn from their experiences and approaches.

- Keep a journal or document your coding experiments and reflections.

- Set aside dedicated time for exploration and side projects.

- Embrace failure as a learning opportunity and don't be afraid to take risks.

- Practice mindfulness and embrace a balance between work and leisure.

Remember, curiosity and creativity are not innate traits but skills that can be developed and nurtured over time. By embracing a growth mindset, seeking new experiences, and staying open to learning, you can cultivate curiosity and creativity in programming, enabling you to become a better programmer and problem solver.

Conclusion

Cultivating curiosity and creativity in programming is essential for unlocking our full potential as programmers. By embracing a growth mindset, fostering a creative environment, engaging in cross-training activities, and following practical tips, we can continuously enhance our ability to think critically, explore new ideas, and find innovative solutions to programming challenges. Let us embrace curiosity and creativity as we continue our programming journey, inspired by the legacy of Dennis Ritchie.

The responsibility of programmers to carry on Ritchie's legacy

As we reflect on the impact and contributions of Dennis Ritchie, it becomes clear that his work has left an indelible mark on the field of programming. The C language, his most significant creation, continues to be widely used and forms the foundation for numerous software systems and applications. To honor Ritchie's legacy and ensure the continued progress of programming, it is the responsibility of programmers today to carry forward his principles of innovation, collaboration, and practicality.

4.2.5.1 Emphasizing the importance of simplicity and elegance

One of the fundamental aspects of Ritchie's work that programmers should carry forward is the emphasis on simplicity and elegance in programming. The C language itself embodies these principles, with its minimalist syntax and concise yet expressive constructs. As programmers, we must strive to write code that is clean, readable, and maintainable, following the principle of "keep it simple, stupid" (KISS). This means avoiding unnecessary complexity, excessive dependencies, and convoluted logic.

To illustrate this, let's consider an example. Suppose we are tasked with writing a program to calculate the average of a list of numbers. Instead of writing convoluted code with unnecessary loops and conditionals, we can leverage the simplicity of the C language to achieve the same result more elegantly:

```
\# include <stdio.h>

float calculate_average(int numbers[], int length) {
    int sum = 0;
    for (int i = 0; i < length; i++) {
        sum += numbers[i];
    }
    return (float) sum / length;
}

int main() {
    int numbers[] = { 2, 4, 6, 8, 10 };
    int length = sizeof(numbers) / sizeof(numbers[0]);
    float average = calculate_average(numbers, length);
    printf("The average is: %.2f\n", average);
    return 0;
}
```

By keeping our code simple and concise, we enhance readability and maintainability, making it easier for ourselves and others to understand and build upon our work.

4.2.5.2 Encouraging a culture of collaboration and knowledge sharing

Another key aspect of Dennis Ritchie's legacy is his collaboration with Ken Thompson and his efforts to build a culture of collaboration at Bell Labs. As programmers, it is our responsibility to continue fostering a collaborative environment and to actively engage in knowledge sharing.

Collaboration allows us to leverage the collective expertise and creativity of a diverse group of individuals. By working together, we can solve complex problems more effectively, share ideas, and learn from one another's experiences. This can be achieved through open-source projects, online communities, and participation in professional networking events.

Furthermore, we should make a conscious effort to share knowledge and contribute to the programming community. This can be done through writing informative blog posts, creating tutorials, conducting workshops, or engaging in mentorship programs. By actively sharing our knowledge and experiences, we contribute to the growth and development of future generations of programmers.

4.2.5.3 Pursuing continuous learning and exploration

Dennis Ritchie was not only a brilliant programmer but also a lifelong learner. Throughout his career, he continuously explored new ideas, concepts, and technologies. As programmers, we have a responsibility to emulate Ritchie's spirit of curiosity and embrace lifelong learning.

To stay relevant and keep pace with the rapidly evolving technological landscape, we must continuously update our skills and explore emerging programming paradigms, languages, and frameworks. This can be achieved through reading technical articles, attending conferences, participating in online courses, or experimenting with personal projects.

By embracing lifelong learning, we not only equip ourselves with the latest tools and techniques but also foster a mindset of growth and adaptability. This enables us to tackle new challenges, push the boundaries of what is possible, and build upon Ritchie's legacy of innovation.

4.2.5.4 Ethical considerations and social responsibility

As programmers, we must recognize the ethical considerations and social responsibility that come with our work. The technology we build has a profound impact on society, and it is our responsibility to ensure that it is used for the collective good.

We should adhere to ethical coding practices, such as respecting user privacy, ensuring data security, and avoiding biases in algorithms. Additionally, we must be mindful of the potential social implications of our code, making efforts to mitigate harm and promote inclusivity and diversity.

By incorporating ethical considerations into our programming practices, we can create technology that benefits society as a whole and upholds the principles that Dennis Ritchie held dear.

In conclusion, as programmers, we have a responsibility to carry on Dennis Ritchie's legacy by emphasizing simplicity and elegance in our code, fostering a culture of collaboration and knowledge sharing, pursuing continuous learning and exploration, and embracing ethical considerations and social responsibility. By doing so, we not only honor Ritchie's contributions but also contribute to the advancement and positive impact of the programming community. It is through our collective efforts that we can build upon the foundations laid by Ritchie and shape the future of programming.

The industry's debt to Dennis Ritchie

Recognizing Ritchie's Contributions to the Software Industry

Dennis Ritchie was an extraordinary individual whose contributions to the software industry revolutionized the field of computer science. His pioneering work in the development of the C language and Unix operating system laid the foundation for modern computing and continues to shape the industry to this day. In this section, we will explore Ritchie's significant contributions and their lasting impact on the software industry.

4.3.1.1 The Birth of the C Language

One of Dennis Ritchie's most notable contributions to the software industry was the birth of the C programming language. In the early 1970s, Ritchie, along with his colleague Ken Thompson, embarked on a quest to create a language that would improve upon the limitations of existing programming languages.

Ritchie's vision was to develop a language that balanced low-level control with high-level abstractions. The result was the C language, which combined the elegance of high-level languages like ALGOL with the efficiency and flexibility of low-level languages like assembly.

The C language introduced several groundbreaking concepts that transformed software development. It introduced a standard set of data types, control structures, and syntax, making it easier to write portable and efficient code. Moreover, it presented a simple, yet powerful, approach to memory management, allowing programmers to directly manipulate system resources.

4.3.1.2 The Significance of the C Language in the Software Industry

Ritchie's creation of the C language had a profound impact on the software industry. Prior to C, programming languages were highly specialized and tied to particular hardware or operating systems. With the advent of C, software development became platform-independent, paving the way for the development of cross-platform applications.

The C language's simplicity, expressiveness, and efficiency made it an ideal choice for system programming, leading to its rapid adoption within the industry. Its portability and versatility played a vital role in the proliferation of operating systems, compilers, and libraries, enabling the development of complex software systems.

Furthermore, the C language served as a catalyst for the creation of numerous programming languages that built upon its foundations. Languages such as C++, Objective-C, and C# owe their existence to the pioneering work of Dennis Ritchie.

The influence of the C language on modern programming languages cannot be overstated.

4.3.1.3 Standardization Efforts and Language Evolution

In addition to creating the C language, Ritchie played an instrumental role in standardizing and evolving the language. He actively participated in the development of standardized versions of the C language, ensuring its consistent implementation across different compilers and platforms.

Ritchie's commitment to language evolution led to the publication of multiple versions of the C language with improved features and enhanced compatibility. His efforts resulted in the ANSI C standard, which solidified the language's syntax and semantics and provided a common foundation for software development.

4.3.1.4 Influence on the Business of Software

Ritchie's contributions to the software industry extended beyond the technical aspects of programming languages. His work had a significant impact on the business of software as well. The portability and efficiency of the C language made it an attractive choice for software companies looking to develop and market their products across multiple platforms.

The availability of high-quality compilers and libraries for the C language meant that software projects could be developed more rapidly and cost-effectively. This acceleration in development cycles allowed companies to bring their products to market faster, giving them a competitive edge.

Moreover, Ritchie's focus on simplicity and efficiency in the design of the C language influenced the philosophy of software development. The concept of "doing more with less" became ingrained in the industry, leading to the development of leaner and more efficient software systems.

4.3.1.5 Recognizing Ritchie's Contributions

Dennis Ritchie's contributions to the software industry have been widely recognized and honored. In 1983, he was awarded the Turing Award, the highest honor in computer science, for his work on the development of the C language and Unix operating system. This prestigious accolade acknowledged the immense impact of his contributions on the field.

Beyond the Turing Award, Ritchie received numerous other awards and honors throughout his career, further underscoring the significance of his work. His contributions continue to be celebrated within the programming community and academia, cementing his place as one of the most influential figures in the history of computer science.

It is crucial for industry leaders and developers to recognize Ritchie's contributions and strive to preserve and build upon his legacy. By continuing to innovate and develop software solutions that adhere to the principles set forth by

Ritchie, the industry can honor his work and ensure the ongoing relevance and longevity of the C language.

4.3.1.6 Balancing Tradition and Innovation

While recognizing Ritchie's contributions, it is vital for the software industry to strike a balance between tradition and innovation. The stability and widespread use of the C language should not hinder the exploration of new programming paradigms and languages. Instead, Ritchie's legacy should serve as a foundation for inspiring further innovation and creativity in programming.

By embracing Ritchie's spirit of collaboration, simplicity, and efficiency, programmers can push the boundaries of software development while respecting the principles that have stood the test of time. In doing so, they can honor Ritchie's contributions to the software industry and create a future that builds upon his remarkable legacy.

In conclusion, Dennis Ritchie's contributions to the software industry, particularly with the creation of the C language, have paved the way for modern computing and transformed the field of computer science. The significance and impact of his work are recognized and celebrated both within the programming community and through prestigious awards. By acknowledging and honoring Ritchie's contributions, fostering innovation, and continuing to build upon his principles, the software industry can ensure the lasting relevance of his work and carry forward his spirit of innovation and collaboration into the future.

Honoring Ritchie through continued innovation

As the world of programming continues to evolve, it is crucial to honor the contributions of Dennis Ritchie by embracing continued innovation. Ritchie's work laid the foundation for modern software development, and by building upon his principles, we can push the boundaries of what is possible in programming. In this section, we will explore different ways in which Ritchie's legacy can inspire and guide programmers to pursue innovative solutions.

Adopting a problem-solving mindset

One of the key aspects of Ritchie's work was his ability to solve complex problems by approaching them with a clear and focused mindset. To honor his legacy, programmers should strive to cultivate a problem-solving mindset in their work. This includes actively seeking out challenges, thinking critically, and exploring unconventional solutions.

For example, consider the problem of optimizing code execution. Programmers can draw inspiration from Ritchie's innovative approach to performance enhancements, such as the creation of the C language itself. By studying Ritchie's principles and techniques, programmers can develop a deep understanding of how to improve efficiency and maximize performance.

Exploring new programming paradigms

Ritchie's C language was revolutionary in its simplicity and versatility, offering a new programming paradigm that focused on control and efficiency. To honor his legacy, programmers should continue to explore new programming paradigms that push the boundaries of what is possible.

Functional programming, for instance, is a paradigm that treats computation as the evaluation of mathematical functions and avoids changing state and mutable data. By embracing functional programming concepts, programmers can harness the power of simplicity and expressiveness, just like Ritchie did with the C language.

Additionally, the rise of artificial intelligence and machine learning presents another opportunity for honoring Ritchie's legacy through innovation. As these fields continue to evolve, programmers can contribute by combining their knowledge of the C language, functional programming, and other relevant paradigms to develop intelligent algorithms and systems.

Embracing open-source collaboration

Ritchie's collaboration with Ken Thompson on the development of Unix exemplifies the power of open-source collaboration. To honor his legacy, programmers should embrace the spirit of collaboration and contribute to open-source projects.

Open-source software allows programmers from all over the world to collaborate and enhance each other's work. By actively participating in open-source projects, programmers can not only pay tribute to Ritchie's collaborative approach but also continue to push the boundaries of innovation.

Moreover, open-source projects provide valuable learning opportunities and foster a sense of community among programmers. By sharing code, knowledge, and experience, programmers can collectively solve complex challenges and drive further innovation.

Mentoring future generations

To truly honor Ritchie's legacy, it is essential to inspire and mentor future generations of programmers. By passing on knowledge and providing guidance, experienced programmers can shape the next wave of innovative thinkers.

Mentoring can take many forms, from teaching programming concepts to sharing real-world experiences and challenges. Through mentorship, programmers can help cultivate curiosity, creativity, and a problem-solving mindset in aspiring programmers, ensuring that Ritchie's legacy lives on.

Additionally, mentorship can foster a sense of community and collaboration, creating an environment in which new ideas can flourish. By dedicating time and effort to mentorship, programmers can contribute directly to the continued innovation in programming.

Pushing the boundaries of technology

Lastly, to honor Ritchie's legacy, programmers must continuously strive to push the boundaries of technology.   This includes exploring emerging technologies, experimenting with new tools and frameworks, and staying up-to-date with the latest advancements in the field.

For instance, the rapid growth of cloud computing, Internet of Things (IoT), and blockchain technology presents opportunities for innovation. Programmers can leverage these technologies to develop groundbreaking applications and systems that address real-world problems.

Furthermore, as technology becomes more intertwined with various industries, programmers can contribute to the digital transformation by applying their skills and knowledge to reshape traditional processes and systems.

In conclusion, honoring Ritchie's legacy through continued innovation requires adopting a problem-solving mindset, exploring new programming paradigms, embracing open-source collaboration, mentoring future generations, and pushing the boundaries of technology.   By following in Ritchie's footsteps and building upon his principles, programmers can ensure that his contributions to the world of programming live on and continue to shape the future.

The role of industry leaders in preserving Ritchie's legacy

Industry leaders have a crucial role to play in preserving the legacy of Dennis Ritchie. As the torchbearers of the software industry, they have the responsibility to ensure that Ritchie's contributions to the field of computer science are not forgotten and that his ideas continue to shape and influence the future of programming. In this section, we will explore the various ways in which industry leaders can honor Ritchie's work and keep his memory alive.

Setting Standards and Best Practices

One of the most effective ways for industry leaders to preserve Ritchie's legacy is by establishing and promoting standards and best practices inspired by his work. The C language, developed by Ritchie, served as the foundation for numerous programming languages and systems. By adopting and advocating for the use of C and its principles, industry leaders can ensure that Ritchie's ideas remain relevant and continue to guide the development of software.

Furthermore, by setting standards for coding conventions, documentation, and software development processes, industry leaders can help maintain the integrity and quality of programming practices. Just as Ritchie emphasized the importance of simplicity and clarity in code, industry leaders must instill these values in their organizations and promote them industry-wide. This not only pays tribute to Ritchie's legacy but also helps create a more cohesive and efficient software development ecosystem.

Investing in Education and Research

Another crucial aspect of preserving Ritchie's legacy is investing in education and research. Industry leaders have the resources and influence to support educational initiatives that teach the C language and its core concepts. By providing funding, scholarships, and mentorship opportunities, they can ensure that future generations of programmers learn about Ritchie's contributions and can build upon his work.

Additionally, industry leaders can support research efforts that explore the evolution and impact of the C language, as well as its continued relevance in modern software development. By funding research projects, creating partnerships with academic institutions, and encouraging collaboration between industry and academia, they can facilitate a deeper understanding of Ritchie's ideas and their practical applications.

Promoting Open Source and Collaboration

Dennis Ritchie's collaboration with Ken Thompson on the development of Unix embodies the essence of open-source software. Industry leaders can honor Ritchie's legacy by promoting the ideals of open-source and fostering a culture of collaboration within their organizations and the wider programming community.

Creating platforms and opportunities for programmers to share their code, knowledge, and expertise not only preserves the spirit of collaboration that was central to Ritchie's work but also allows for the continued growth and improvement of software development practices. By embracing open-source principles and encouraging their employees to contribute to open-source projects, industry leaders can pay tribute to Ritchie's legacy while also nurturing innovation and creativity within the industry.

Supporting Diversity and Inclusion

Dennis Ritchie's contributions to computer science are a testament to the power of diverse perspectives and inclusive environments. Industry leaders must recognize the importance of diversity and inclusion in driving innovation and progress. By creating inclusive workplaces and supporting initiatives that promote diversity in the field of programming, industry leaders can honor Ritchie's legacy by ensuring that his vision of a vibrant and inclusive community of programmers continues to thrive.

Through mentorship programs, scholarships for underrepresented groups, and initiatives that address the gender and diversity gap in tech, industry leaders can actively contribute to a more inclusive programming landscape. By providing equal opportunities and fostering an environment where everyone's ideas are valued, they can help carry forward Ritchie's spirit of collaboration and openness.

Preserving and Documenting Ritchie's Contributions

Lastly, industry leaders have a responsibility to preserve and document Ritchie's contributions for future generations. This can be done through initiatives such as creating archives, organizing conferences or workshops focused on Ritchie's work, and supporting projects that aim to collect and preserve historical artifacts related to his endeavors.

By documenting Ritchie's ideas, innovations, and the development process of the C language and Unix, industry leaders can ensure that his work remains accessible and available for study and reference. This allows programmers to understand the evolution of programming languages and systems, gain insights into Ritchie's problem-solving approach, and draw inspiration from his solutions.

In conclusion, industry leaders play a crucial role in preserving Dennis Ritchie's legacy. By setting standards, investing in education and research, promoting open source and collaboration, supporting diversity and inclusion, and preserving and documenting Ritchie's contributions, they can ensure that his ideas continue to shape the field of computer science. In doing so, they not only honor Ritchie's memory but also contribute to the ongoing evolution and advancement of programming.

The impact of Ritchie on the business of software

Dennis Ritchie's contributions to the business of software have had a profound impact on the industry. His work, particularly the development of the C language and Unix operating system, revolutionized the way software was created, distributed, and commercialized. In this section, we will explore the various ways in which Ritchie's innovations shaped the business landscape of software.

Building a foundation for commercial software

Ritchie's creation of the C language played a pivotal role in the development of commercial software. Prior to C, programming languages were often hardware-dependent, which limited their portability and made software development a complex and costly endeavor. C provided a solution to this problem by introducing a higher-level programming language that abstracted away hardware-specific details.

The C language's machine-independent nature allowed software developers to write code that could be easily compiled and executed on different hardware architectures. This significantly reduced the effort required to port software to different platforms, enabling software vendors to reach a much larger market. As a result, the commercial software industry experienced explosive growth, with companies able to develop and sell applications to a wider range of customers.

Enabling software standardization

Another important impact of Ritchie's work on the business of software was the promotion of software standardization. Before C, there was a lack of standardized programming languages, leading to fragmentation and vendor lock-in. This created obstacles for software developers and impeded the interoperability of software systems.

Ritchie's creation of the C language, along with his contributions to standardization efforts, helped establish a common programming language that could be adopted by multiple vendors. This not only facilitated collaboration among developers from different organizations but also encouraged the development of third-party libraries and tools. The availability of these standardized resources made it easier for businesses to build software solutions, reducing development time and costs.

Fostering the growth of software ecosystems

Ritchie's work on the Unix operating system played a key role in fostering the growth of software ecosystems. Unix introduced the concept of modular software development, where small, focused programs could be combined to create more complex applications. This approach encouraged collaboration and code sharing among developers, leading to the creation of a rich ecosystem of Unix applications and utilities.

The Unix philosophy of "do one thing and do it well" resonated with software developers, who recognized the benefits of reusability and simplicity. This philosophy contributed to the rise of the open-source movement, where software source code is made freely available for anyone to use, modify, and distribute. Open-source software became a catalyst for innovation, empowering businesses to leverage the collective expertise of a global community of developers.

Transforming business models

Ritchie's contributions also had a significant impact on software business models. The open-source nature of Unix, along with the popularity of the C language, enabled new ways of distributing and monetizing software. Instead of relying solely on closed, proprietary systems, companies began to embrace open-source software and adopt different revenue models.

One such model is the freemium approach, where a basic version of the software is provided for free, and premium features or support are offered for a fee. This model allows businesses to attract a large user base, gain market share, and generate revenue from value-added services. The availability of open-source tools and libraries further reduced the cost of development, making it more feasible for startups and small businesses to enter the software market.

Additionally, the success of open-source software demonstrated the value of community-driven development and collaboration. Businesses began to realize the benefits of contributing to open-source projects, leveraging the collective effort and expertise of developers worldwide. By participating in open-source communities, companies not only improved their reputation but also gained access to a talent pool of highly skilled programmers.

Cultivating a culture of innovation

Perhaps one of the most significant impacts of Ritchie on the business of software is his role in cultivating a culture of innovation. His work inspired generations of programmers to think creatively, challenge conventions, and push the boundaries of what was possible in software development.

Ritchie's emphasis on simplicity and elegance in programming influenced not only the design of software systems but also the approach to problem-solving. His contributions to software engineering and his collaborative work with Ken Thompson at Bell Labs set a standard for excellence that continues to be admired and emulated by programmers around the world.

The business of software owes a great debt to Dennis Ritchie. His innovations, such as the C language and Unix operating system, transformed the industry by enabling software standardization, fostering the growth of software ecosystems, transforming business models, and inspiring a culture of innovation. As the legacy of Ritchie continues to shape the future of software, it is our responsibility as programmers and industry leaders to carry forward his spirit of creativity, collaboration, and relentless pursuit of excellence.

Ensuring the longevity of the C language and its principles

Preserving the historical significance

As we celebrate the enduring legacy of Dennis Ritchie and the impact of the C language, it is essential to ensure the longevity of this influential programming language and its principles. To achieve this, we must strive to preserve its historical significance and honor Ritchie's contributions to the software industry.

One way to accomplish this is by documenting the history of the C language and its development, highlighting its pivotal role in shaping modern computing. This documentation can take the form of books, articles, and online resources that detail Ritchie's journey and the impact of his work. By sharing these resources with current and future programmers, we can ensure that the historical context and importance of the C language are not forgotten over time.

Furthermore, it is crucial to preserve artifacts and materials related to the development and evolution of the C language. This could involve archiving source code, documentation, and other relevant materials in digital repositories or dedicated museums. By doing so, we create an invaluable resource for researchers, historians, and programmers, allowing them to understand and learn from the early stages of programming language development.

Nurturing the C language community

To ensure the longevity of the C language, it is vital to nurture a vibrant and active community of C programmers. Such a community can serve as a platform for knowledge sharing, collaboration, and the evolution of the language.

One way to foster this community is through the organization of conferences, workshops, and meetups specifically focused on the C language. These events provide opportunities for programmers to network, exchange ideas, and showcase their expertise. Moreover, these gatherings serve as a platform for introducing new generations of programmers to the C language, helping to sustain its relevance and popularity.

Online forums, mailing lists, and dedicated websites can also play a significant role in nurturing the C language community. These platforms enable programmers from all around the world to connect, seek help, and share insights. By actively participating in these online communities, programmers can contribute to the collective knowledge and ensure that the C language remains a vibrant and collaborative ecosystem.

Supporting education and training

A critical aspect of ensuring the longevity of the C language is through education and training. Providing comprehensive resources and opportunities for programmers to learn and enhance their C language skills is essential for its continued relevance.

Educational institutions, both at the school and university level, should continue offering courses in the C language. These courses should not only cover the fundamentals of the language but also delve into its historical context, principles, and best practices. By incorporating the C language into the curriculum, we can guarantee the next generation of programmers continues to appreciate its value and understand its impact on computer science.

Beyond formal education, organizations and industry leaders should support C language training programs and initiatives. Offering scholarships, grants, and mentorship opportunities can enable aspiring programmers to learn and excel in the C language. By investing in continuous learning and developing the skill set of C programmers, we create a sustainable ecosystem that ensures the principles and ideas behind the C language continue to thrive.

Evolution and adaptation

While preserving the historical significance and nurturing a strong community are essential, it is equally important to embrace the evolution and adaptation of the C language. To ensure its longevity, the language must remain relevant to the changing needs and demands of the software industry.

Maintaining an open-source environment and encouraging contributions from the community allows the C language to evolve organically. This approach promotes innovation, fosters collaboration, and ensures that the language remains attractive to programmers and industry professionals.

Additionally, it is crucial to keep pace with technological advancements and industry trends. Integrating new features, tools, and frameworks into the C language ecosystem enables programmers to utilize modern techniques while still benefiting from the language's simplicity and efficiency. This constant evolution ensures that the C language retains its position as a powerful and versatile programming tool.

Preservation of values and principles

As we look to ensure the longevity of the C language, it is essential to preserve its core values and principles. The simplicity, efficiency, and portability that have defined the C language from its inception must be safeguarded.

Developers should prioritize writing clean, concise, and well-structured code that follows established programming practices. Emphasizing these principles not only results in efficient and maintainable code but also reflects the spirit of the C language itself.

Moreover, it is essential to encourage a culture of learning from existing codebases and openly sharing knowledge. By studying and understanding well-established C projects, programmers can gain insights into effective coding techniques and architectural patterns. This practice not only upholds the fundamental principles of the C language but also fosters a sense of community and collaboration.

Conclusion

Ensuring the longevity of the C language and its principles requires a multifaceted approach. By preserving its historical significance, nurturing the community, supporting education and training, embracing evolution and adaptation, and preserving its core values and principles, we can guarantee that future generations will continue to benefit from and build upon Dennis Ritchie's remarkable contributions to the world of programming. As we move forward, let us remember that the C language is more than just a programming language; it is a testament to the creativity, ingenuity, and collaborative spirit of the programming community.

Conclusion

The enduring legacy of Dennis Ritchie

Reflecting on Ritchie's impact and contributions

Dennis Ritchie's impact on the field of computer science cannot be overstated. Through his groundbreaking work on the development of the C language and the Unix operating system, Ritchie revolutionized software development, laid the foundation for modern programming languages, and changed the way we interact with computers. His contributions continue to shape the industry to this day.

Ritchie's most significant contribution was undoubtedly the creation of the C language. Prior to C, programming languages were complex and difficult to use, often tied to specific hardware platforms. C, with its simple syntax and powerful capabilities, introduced a new era of programming. It provided the abstraction needed to write machine-independent code, allowing developers to write programs that could be easily ported across different systems.

The impact of C on the software industry cannot be overstated. The development of the C compiler made it easier for programmers to write and debug their code, accelerating the software development process. C's influence extended beyond its own language, inspiring the creation of many other programming languages, including C++, Java, and Python. These languages inherited C's syntax and concepts, ensuring the continued relevance and influence of Ritchie's ideas.

Furthermore, Ritchie played a crucial role in standardization efforts within the programming community. His contributions to the American National Standards Institute (ANSI) C committee helped establish C as a widely accepted and standardized language. This standardization provided a solid foundation for the development of portable software and ensured the compatibility of C code across different platforms.

In addition to his work on the C language, Ritchie's role in the creation and

127

development of the Unix operating system cannot be ignored. Unix represented a paradigm shift in operating system design, introducing concepts such as hierarchical file systems, process control, and inter-process communication. It laid the groundwork for modern operating systems and was instrumental in the growth of the open-source movement.

Ritchie's collaboration with Ken Thompson at Bell Labs was key to the success of both C and Unix. Together, they built a culture of collaboration and innovation, inspiring a new generation of programmers to work together towards common goals. Their partnership exemplified the power of teamwork and laid the foundation for future collaborations in the software industry.

Despite facing numerous challenges and obstacles, Ritchie's persistence and innovative spirit allowed him to overcome them and leave a lasting impact. He navigated limited resources and technology constraints to create groundbreaking tools and systems. He competed against industry giants and overcame criticism and skepticism, proving the worth and practicality of his ideas. Ritchie's ability to balance innovation with practicality ensured the widespread adoption and longevity of his contributions.

Ritchie's impact can be seen not only in the realm of computer science but also in academia. The C language became a staple in computer science curricula, providing students with a solid foundation in programming. Understanding Ritchie's contributions and the principles behind the C language is crucial for aspiring programmers, as it helps them grasp fundamental concepts that underpin modern software development.

Moreover, Ritchie's work on Unix influenced the design of subsequent operating systems and the development of distributed computing. Concepts such as process communication and file management continue to shape the landscape of operating systems today. The legacy of Unix can be seen in popular operating systems such as Linux and macOS, showcasing the enduring relevance of Ritchie's ideas.

Ritchie's contributions continue to inspire future generations of programmers. His emphasis on collaboration, innovation, and practicality serves as a guiding principle for software development. Educators recognize the importance of training students in the C language, ensuring a deep understanding of programming history and fostering curiosity and creativity in programming.

As the industry reflects on the impact of Ritchie's work, industry leaders must honor his contributions by continuing to innovate and push the boundaries of software development. Preserving Ritchie's legacy requires ongoing dedication to the principles he espoused, such as simplicity, portability, and reliability. By embracing these principles, programmers can ensure the longevity of the C language and its principles, securing a foundation for future innovation.

In conclusion, Dennis Ritchie's impact on computer science is immeasurable. Through his creation of the C language and his work on Unix, Ritchie revolutionized software development, inspired generations of programmers, and laid the foundation for modern operating systems and programming languages. His contributions continue to shape the industry, and his legacy serves as a reminder of the power of collaboration, innovation, and practicality. It is the responsibility of programmers to carry forward Ritchie's spirit of excellence and continue to push the boundaries of software development, ensuring a bright future for the field.

The ongoing relevance of the C language

The C programming language, created by Dennis Ritchie, has stood the test of time and continues to be widely used and relevant in the modern computing landscape. Despite being developed almost five decades ago, the C language remains a cornerstone of software development, with its influence extending far beyond its initial intended purpose. In this section, we will explore the ongoing relevance of the C language and the reasons why it continues to be an essential tool for programmers.

Efficiency and Portability

One of the key reasons for the continued popularity of the C language is its efficiency and portability. C allows programmers to write code that is close to the machine-level, providing control over hardware resources and enabling optimization for performance-critical applications. This low-level ability to manipulate memory, perform bitwise operations, and access hardware directly makes C an ideal choice for system programming, embedded systems, and other resource-constrained environments.

Moreover, C is highly portable, with compilers available for various platforms and operating systems. This allows C programs to be easily migrated from one platform to another, making it a versatile language for cross-platform development. The portability of C is further enhanced by its standardized syntax and libraries, ensuring that code written in C can be easily understood and compiled on different systems.

Close-to-the-hardware Programming

In today's computing landscape, where high-level languages offer increased productivity and abstraction, the need for close-to-the-hardware programming is still prevalent. Certain applications, such as operating systems, device drivers, and real-time systems, require direct control over hardware resources to achieve the desired functionality and performance. This is where the C language excels.

By providing direct access to memory, pointers, and other low-level constructs, C allows programmers to write code that intimately interacts with the hardware. This level of control is often critical in situations where performance optimizations, hardware-specific features, or fine-grained memory management are required.

Legacy Systems and Codebase

Another reason for the ongoing relevance of the C language is its prevalence in legacy systems and codebases. Many critical applications, such as operating systems, databases, and network protocols, were originally written in C or C++, which makes the ability to read, understand, and maintain existing code written in C a valuable skill.

As businesses and organizations continue to rely on these legacy systems, the need for programmers who can understand and work with C code remains high. In fact, the scarcity of skilled C programmers has created a demand for professionals who can maintain and update these systems, ensuring their continued functionality and security.

Interfacing with Other Programming Languages

C serves as a bridge between high-level programming languages and low-level systems. Its ability to interface with other languages, such as C++, Python, and Java, allows programmers to leverage C's performance advantages while benefiting from the productivity and ease-of-use of higher-level languages.

For instance, many popular software libraries and frameworks, such as the Python's NumPy and SciPy libraries, utilize C extensions to achieve high computational performance. These extensions provide a seamless integration between Python and C, enabling the best of both worlds - the simplicity and expressiveness of Python, combined with the performance optimizations of C.

Teaching Fundamental Programming Concepts

The C language also plays a significant role in education, especially in computer science and programming curricula. Its simplicity and straightforward syntax make it an excellent tool for teaching fundamental programming concepts, such as variables, loops, conditionals, and functions.

By starting with C, students gain a deep understanding of how programs are executed, memory management, and the inner workings of a computer system. This forms a solid foundation upon which they can build their knowledge of higher-level languages and more complex programming paradigms.

Cultivating a Strong Problem-Solving Mindset

Lastly, the ongoing relevance of the C language lies in its ability to cultivate a strong problem-solving mindset in programmers. Due to its low-level nature, C forces programmers to think critically about memory management, algorithmic efficiency, and program optimization.

By working with C, programmers develop a strong understanding of program execution and gain insights into performance trade-offs. This mindset of delving into the core of a problem and seeking optimal solutions carries over to other programming languages and has a lasting impact on a programmer's approach to problem-solving.

In conclusion, the C programming language continues to be relevant in today's computing landscape due to its efficiency, portability, and close-to-the-hardware capabilities. Its prevalence in legacy systems, ability to interface with other programming languages, and educational value further contribute to its ongoing importance. Moreover, C cultivates a strong problem-solving mindset, making it a powerful tool for programmers. As the field of computing continues to evolve, the lessons learned from C and the principles it embodies will remain invaluable for current and future generations of programmers.

Ritchie's influence on programming culture

Dennis Ritchie's contributions to programming culture have left an indelible impact on the way programmers think, work, and collaborate. His ideas and concepts have shaped not just the C language and its evolution, but also the broader field of computer science and software development.

The pragmatic approach to programming

One of the key aspects of Ritchie's influence on programming culture is his pragmatic approach. Ritchie believed in building practical solutions that could be easily understood, implemented, and maintained. This philosophy is reflected in the design of the C language itself, which emphasizes simplicity, efficiency, and code readability.

Ritchie's focus on practicality has resonated with programmers worldwide, leading to the widespread adoption of the C language. The C language's straightforward syntax and low-level control have made it a preferred choice for systems programming, embedded systems, and performance-critical applications. Through his emphasis on practicality, Ritchie has influenced generations of programmers to prioritize simplicity, efficiency, and maintainability in their code.

Encouraging collaboration and knowledge sharing

Ritchie's influence on programming culture extends beyond his technical contributions. He was a strong advocate for collaboration and knowledge sharing among programmers. This can be seen in his collaborations with Ken Thompson, his partnership with Bell Labs, and his contributions to the development of the UNIX operating system.

Ritchie understood the value of collaboration in advancing the field of computer science. He actively promoted the exchange of ideas, insights, and expertise among programmers, fostering an environment of open communication and cooperation. This culture of collaboration has had a lasting impact on programming culture, shaping the way programmers collaborate, learn from each other, and contribute to open-source projects.

Promoting portability and compatibility

Another aspect of Ritchie's influence on programming culture is his emphasis on portability and compatibility. The C language was designed to be portable across different hardware platforms, allowing programs written in C to be easily adapted to run on different systems. This portability has been crucial in enabling software developers to create cross-platform applications and systems.

Ritchie's focus on compatibility also played a significant role in the success of the C language. The C language's compatibility with assembly language made it accessible to systems programmers familiar with low-level programming. Additionally, the compatibility of C with other languages, such as C++, has facilitated the integration and reuse of existing codebases, promoting code interoperability and reducing development time.

Inspiring a culture of continuous learning

Throughout his career, Ritchie demonstrated a deep commitment to continuous learning and innovation. He constantly sought new challenges, explored new ideas, and pushed the boundaries of programming. His curiosity and drive for knowledge continue to inspire programmers to embrace a culture of continuous learning.

Ritchie's approach to programming culture encourages programmers to stay updated with the latest developments in technology, explore new programming languages and paradigms, and to never stop learning. He serves as a role model for embracing intellectual curiosity and using it to drive innovation and personal growth.

Legacy in modern programming languages

Ritchie's influence on programming culture can be seen in the evolution of modern programming languages. Many subsequent languages, such as C++, Java, and Python, have been influenced by the syntax, features, and principles of the C language.

The C language's focus on efficiency, modularity, and control has become a cornerstone of modern programming languages. The legacy of the C language can be seen in the widespread use of structured programming principles, the adoption of modular programming techniques, and the emphasis on code readability and maintainability.

Ritchie's influence on programming culture extends beyond the C language itself. His pragmatic approach, emphasis on collaboration and knowledge sharing, focus on portability and compatibility, and commitment to continuous learning have left a lasting imprint on the way programmers approach their work.

In conclusion, Dennis Ritchie's influence on programming culture is profound and far-reaching. By championing a pragmatic approach, encouraging collaboration, promoting portability and compatibility, inspiring continuous learning, and leaving a legacy in modern programming languages, Ritchie has shaped the mindset, values, and practices of programmers worldwide. His contributions continue to impact and guide future generations of programmers, ensuring that his influence on programming culture will endure.

Carrying forward Ritchie's spirit of innovation and collaboration

One of the greatest legacies of Dennis Ritchie is his unwavering spirit of innovation and collaboration. Throughout his career, Ritchie constantly pushed the boundaries of what was possible in programming languages and operating systems, and he did so with a deep sense of collaboration and community. In order to carry forward Ritchie's spirit, it is essential to understand the key principles that drove his work and the lessons we can learn from his approach.

Principle 1: Embrace Openness and Collaboration

Ritchie firmly believed in the power of collaboration and the sharing of knowledge. He understood that innovation thrived when ideas were freely exchanged and when individuals worked together towards a common goal. By embracing openness and collaboration, we can build upon the foundation laid by Ritchie and continue to advance the field of programming.

To carry forward Ritchie's spirit of innovation and collaboration, programmers should actively participate in open-source projects, contribute to online communities, and share their knowledge through blogs, tutorials, and conferences. By doing so, we can foster an environment where ideas are freely exchanged and where the collective wisdom of the community drives progress.

Principle 2: Foster a Culture of Learning

Ritchie was a lifelong learner, always seeking to expand his knowledge and understanding of computer science. He believed that continuous learning was essential for staying at the forefront of innovation. To carry forward Ritchie's spirit, we must foster a culture of learning within the programming community.

Programmers should constantly strive to acquire new skills, explore emerging technologies, and stay informed about the latest developments in the field. This can be achieved through online courses, workshops, and by engaging in peer-to-peer learning. By continuously expanding our knowledge, we can push the boundaries of what is possible and continue to innovate in the spirit of Ritchie.

Principle 3: Balance Practicality and Innovation

Ritchie understood the importance of balancing practicality with innovation. While he was known for his groundbreaking work, he always ensured that his creations were usable and practical in real-world scenarios. This balance between practicality and innovation is a key principle that programmers should carry forward.

In our pursuit of innovation, it is crucial to consider the practical implications and real-world applications of our work. It is not enough to create groundbreaking solutions; we must also ensure that these solutions solve real problems and address the needs of end-users. By adopting Ritchie's approach of balancing practicality and innovation, we can create software that truly makes a difference.

Principle 4: Encourage Diversity and Inclusion

Ritchie recognized the value of diverse perspectives and believed that inclusion was essential for driving innovation. He actively promoted diversity in the programming community and encouraged individuals from different backgrounds and experiences to contribute their ideas and insights.

To carry forward Ritchie's spirit, it is crucial to create an inclusive and diverse environment within the programming community. By embracing diversity, we can harness the power of different perspectives and foster innovation. This can be achieved by supporting initiatives that promote diversity, advocating for equal opportunities, and actively seeking out diverse voices in the field.

Principle 5: Mentor the Next Generation

Ritchie understood the importance of mentorship and believed in the power of guiding and inspiring the next generation of programmers. He recognized that by imparting knowledge and sharing experiences, we can shape the future of programming.

To carry forward Ritchie's spirit, it is crucial to mentor and support aspiring programmers. By sharing our knowledge, providing guidance, and offering opportunities for growth, we can inspire the next generation of innovators. Mentorship can take many forms, such as volunteering at coding workshops, participating in mentorship programs, or offering internships to young programmers.

By embracing these principles and carrying forward Ritchie's spirit of innovation and collaboration, we can honor his legacy and ensure that the field of programming continues to thrive. It is through openness, learning, practicality, diversity, and mentorship that we can push the boundaries of what is possible and create a future that Dennis Ritchie would be proud of.

Example: Collaborative Open-Source Project

To put these principles into practice, let's consider an example of a collaborative open-source project that carries forward Ritchie's spirit.

Imagine a group of programmers coming together to create a new programming language, inspired by C but with modern features and improved usability. This open-source project would embrace collaboration, allowing developers from around the world to contribute their ideas and insights. By fostering a culture of learning, the project would also provide resources and documentation to help programmers understand the language and contribute effectively.

The project would balance practicality and innovation by addressing real-world programming challenges and implementing new features that enhance productivity and efficiency. It would also actively seek out contributions from diverse voices, ensuring that the language reflects the needs and perspectives of a wide range of programmers.

Furthermore, the project would mentor and support aspiring programmers, offering opportunities for them to contribute, learn, and grow. Through mentorship programs and online forums, experienced developers would guide and inspire the next generation.

By following these principles, the collaborative open-source project would embody Ritchie's spirit of innovation and collaboration. It would push the boundaries of programming languages, embrace openness and diversity, and foster a culture of learning. In doing so, it would honor Ritchie's legacy and inspire future generations of programmers.

In conclusion, carrying forward Ritchie's spirit of innovation and collaboration requires embracing openness and collaboration, fostering a culture of learning, balancing practicality and innovation, encouraging diversity and inclusion, and mentoring the next generation of programmers. By following these principles, we can create a future that embodies the values and principles that Dennis Ritchie held dearly. Let us continue to push the boundaries of what is possible, inspire one another, and honor Ritchie's legacy in the ever-evolving world of programming.

The future of programming and the lessons we can learn from Ritchie

As we reflect on the enduring legacy of Dennis Ritchie, it is essential to consider the future of programming and the valuable lessons we can learn from his work. Ritchie's contributions to computer science continue to influence and shape the field, and his ideas remain relevant even in the rapidly evolving landscape of technology. In this section, we will explore the future of programming, the ongoing relevance of the C language, Ritchie's influence on programming culture, and the lessons we can draw from his life and work.

The future of programming

The future of programming holds limitless possibilities, driven by advancements in artificial intelligence, robotics, cloud computing, and quantum computing. As new technologies emerge, programmers will need to adapt and acquire new skills to harness the full potential of these tools. However, amidst these exciting developments, it is essential to remember the timeless principles that Ritchie's work embodies and continues to inspire.

The ongoing relevance of the C language

While programming languages come and go, the C language remains a fundamental pillar of modern software development. Its simplicity, efficiency, and versatility continue to make it an indispensable tool for building robust and efficient systems. As we look to the future, the C language will continue to thrive in low-level programming, embedded systems, and performance-critical applications. Its impact extends beyond the language itself, influencing the design and development of other popular languages such as C++, Objective-C, and Rust.

Ritchie's influence on programming culture

Beyond his technical contributions, Dennis Ritchie left an indelible mark on programming culture. His work embodied a spirit of collaboration, curiosity, and a dedication to elegance and simplicity. These principles continue to inspire programmers to strive for clean, maintainable code that stands the test of time. Ritchie's meticulous attention to detail and his emphasis on practicality over theoretical purity serve as valuable lessons for programmers in any era.

Lessons from Ritchie's life and work

There are several lessons we can learn from Dennis Ritchie's life and work that will guide us into the future of programming:

1. **Simplicity and clarity:** Ritchie's approach to programming emphasized simplicity and clarity. He believed in writing code that is easy to understand, maintain, and debug. As the complexity of software systems grows, it becomes even more critical to prioritize simplicity in our code. By embracing simplicity, we can create more reliable and robust software that is easier to adapt and extend.

2. **Collaboration and teamwork:** Ritchie's success was not achieved in isolation but through collaboration and teamwork. His partnership with Ken Thompson and the culture of collaboration they built at Bell Labs were instrumental in developing groundbreaking technologies like Unix and the C language. As the

future of programming unfolds, teams of programmers will continue to play a crucial role in pushing the boundaries of innovation and creating transformative software.

3. Continuous learning: Ritchie's passion for programming was fueled by his insatiable curiosity and his commitment to continuous learning. In the future, programmers must embrace lifelong learning to keep pace with evolving technologies and emerging trends.   By staying curious and seeking out new knowledge, we can adapt to changing circumstances and remain at the forefront of the programming field.

4. Balancing innovation and practicality: Ritchie understood the importance of balancing innovation with practicality.   While he was at the forefront of revolutionary developments in programming languages and operating systems, his work always prioritized usefulness and real-world impact. This lesson reminds us to consider the practical application of our programming solutions and strive for tangible outcomes that benefit both end-users and the broader community.

5. Preserving Ritchie's legacy: Lastly, as programmers, we have a responsibility to preserve Dennis Ritchie's legacy. This entails honoring his contributions by building upon his ideas, advocating for clean and readable code, and promoting collaboration within the programming community. By carrying forward Ritchie's spirit of innovation and dedication to excellence, we can ensure that his work continues to inspire and shape the future of programming.

In conclusion, the future of programming holds tremendous promise, driven by technological advancements and new paradigms.   However, amidst this evolution, we should take inspiration from Dennis Ritchie and his timeless principles.   By embracing simplicity, collaboration, continuous learning, and a balance between innovation and practicality, we can navigate the future with confidence and honor Ritchie's contributions, ensuring a vibrant and impactful programming landscape.

Index